Roberto Sansón Mizrahi

Adjusting the Course

Getting out of the crisis towards a sustainable development

Opinión Sur Collection

Art work:
Gustavo Oliveira and Mariano Ignacio Padró

Editing:
Susie L. Shuford

English Translation:
Loris Bestani

© 2010, Opinión Sur
ISBN
1450575471
9781450575478

Original Spanish Language Edition published by
Opinión Sur/Del Umbral, Copyright © 2009.

*To my dear friends Monte and Betty Factor,
Peggy Dulany, Pam Solo, Joan Goldsmith, Arthur
Domike and Bruce Schearer*

Table of Contents

About
the Author

Roberto Sansón Mizrahi is an economist and urban and regional planner. He worked in several American and European countries, where he led business and development organizations, such as the Esquel Group in Quito and Washington DC, the South North Development Initiative in New York, Sur Norte Inversión y Desarrollo in Buenos Aires, and RAFAD (Research and Applications for Alternative Financing for Development) in Geneva. In addition, he was a member of Global Partners, a global action team focused on development and the environment. He has a broad international experience in sustainable development, micro-finance, employment generation, and local economic development. He has given courses, workshops and work sessions in Latin America, Africa and Asia. He is the author of the book Un país para todos *and of several publications on inclusive business developers, new ways of promoting local development and the global crisis. Today he lives and works as a consultant in the capital city of Argentina, where he serves as co-editor of Opinion Sur.*

About
Opinión Sur Collection

Adjusting the Course is one of the books that make up the Opinion Sur collection. The aim of this collection is to contribute through strategic thinking and proposals for action to enhancing the development of countries in the Southern Hemisphere. Its analysis and proposals draw on Opinion Sur, a monthly virtual publication distributed in Spanish, English and Portuguese to almost 70.000 subscribers in a wide diversity of countries.

Other Opinion Sur products are the digital publication Opinion Sur Youth, on-line free e-books, weekly newspapers columns and the blog Un país para todos (only in Spanish).

Opinión Sur works in association with the South North Development Initiative and Sur Norte Inversión y Desarrollo, sister organizations based in New York and Buenos Aires.

www.opinionsur.org.ar
www.southnorth.org
www.surnorte.org.ar

Preface

For the past six years, long before the emergence of the contemporary global crisis, our Opinion Sur columns (www.opinionsur.org.ar) analyzed the negative effects of concentrated growth in countries of the Southern Hemisphere. The social cost has been titanic; enormous economic and political exclusion of vast majorities; painful the negative impact on the human condition.

What is appalling and bewildering is that such destruction, such generalized alienation, such disregard for the human being, took place simultaneously with a remarkable scientific and technological development, unprecedented for humanity. Many and diverse factors made this acceleration of scientific discoveries and technological innovations possible: on the one hand, the longstanding and incessant accumulation of knowledge that ended up in the current explosive rate of growth; and, on the other hand, the development of a vigorous productive apparatus that in its way towards globalization was capable of drawing on the scientific and technological knowledge to achieve its own expansion and strengthening.

Depending on how that remarkable potentiality is conducted, it can end up being a blessing or a curse for the planet and those who inhabit it. Well-oriented, it can be transformed into the most powerful and never-imagined development lever; if ill-oriented it could lead to larger unforeseen evils that we could impinge on our precious planet and fellow humans.

Too much to consider, to ponder, to comprehend, when we try to ascertain what we mean by "well" or "ill" orienting the existent, worldwide potential. However, few could question that the addressees of the global effort should be the planet that supports us, and the whole (not just some) of its inhabitants. Such is the essential watershed: what negatively affects our environment and condemns vast majorities of Earth population to a miserable life is clearly part of a destructive orientation of our potential.

Later we would need to clarify in great detail how the environment is today destroyed as well as why the current economic growth is essentially unequal having a few millions of families favored in their material well-being while billion others are left behind or simply excluded.

Any assessment of the current situation and the process generating and reproducing it is based on a heterogeneous substrate of needs, interests, values and emotions that we humans bear precisely as part of our human condition. Therefore, different perspectives exist regarding one reality and highlighting certain aspects of it. The challenge is to wholly comprehend what each perspective expresses, even though it might not necessarily confirm our own worldview; thus, to recognize its contribution, separating the wheat from the chaff, the good from the bad, in sum, learning to talk.

When the global crisis erupted, triggered by the financial system breakdown in affluent countries we focused on identifying which other factors contributed in generating the conditions for such titanic systemic explosion. Searching for comprehension, we drew on what was previously elaborated regarding structural and functional imbalances. We went on publishing at Opinion Sur article after article on different aspects of the crisis in real time as it was evolving. This book gathers those materials with little editing so that readers can follow the painful but enlightening process of the crisis that is still taking place. Economic, sociological, environmental, political, psychological, and ethical issues that seem to run through separate trails converge again as dimensions of a complex, dynamic, and diverse reality. By understanding the effects of the turbulent confluence of needs and interests on the collective survival, a clear need to adjust the course and improve our systemic way of functioning becomes established.

As it usually happens, though the author is an individual, what he publishes builds on diverse contributions. I wish I could thank everyone, but it is impossible as in this day and age the own ideas and opinions are fed by conversations, short notes, televised interviews, informal exchanges with such pace and rate that the rigor to register them all gets diluted. Nevertheless, I do thank those who make Sur Norte Inversion y Desarrollo, Opinion Sur, and South North Development Initiative possible, as with their work, technical assistance and management support facilitated that I could conceive the following lines.

Two very personal experiences rejoice and keep surprising me. First, it is having the privilege of being on the same team with the sociologist and political scientist Patricia Mizrahi, one of my two daughters (Ana Paula lives and is professionally growing abroad). The generational, professional, and gender gap constantly enhances my perception of what is happening while the whirlwind of my grandchildren adds sweetness and extreme pragmatism to my daily life.

With my friend and co-editor of Opinion Sur, Juan Eugenio Corradi, I benefited not only from his vast knowledge and own articles regarding the international crisis (gathered in the e-book *STORM: the ways of the crisis and the ways out of it*), but also from practicing the complex and fascinating task of building in the diversity. It is uncommon to combine knowledge, respect, and irreverent humor; of which Juan Eugenio makes a talented display.

The pain that the crisis brought with it and the bewilderment of seeing the reemergence of solutions not centered in the future of our planet nor its majorities induced us to explore other venues. It was not an easy task to do without resources; but, seen in perspective, it might well be precisely those circumstances what allowed us to depart a few inches from mainstream thinking.

Warm greetings to who will adventure through the following Chapters.

Introduction

If the international economic collapse were only due to the fact that the smooth operation of the economic machinery got blocked, the solution would consist of unblocking what became blocked, and "clearing the way". The pre-existing system would thus be brought back to health and, as it resumes operation, the problems we face today, including extended recession and unemployment, would be solved.

This is, in essence, a functionalist view on the crisis. It should be mentioned that many are the "obstacles" blocking the smooth operation of the economic machinery and, in principle nothing should prevent them from being removed so that we can regain the lost stamina and efficacy. However, this is not easy to accomplish, not only because functional obstacles are too many, but also because they are intimately associated with diverse interests struggling with one another in order to prevail. In any case, it will always be positive to deploy efforts to improve our systemic way of functioning.

Others believe that it was not just the malfunctioning of the economic machinery that caused today's problems but, very especially, the systemic direction that set the course. The economic machinery, which is operated by people and organizations that take care of their individual interests, is heading into a direction prone to produce environmental disasters, serious social conflicts, and acute political instability.

This is a complex issue where economic, political, social and environmental aspects intertwine, involving a large number of factors. Among these, there is a factor that concerns all of us, one which is usually ignored when considering the genesis and development of the current crisis: the alienation in which many of us have fallen as to the significance we attribute to what we are and do. This alienation, which goes beyond the realm of philosophy and individual psychology, projects itself into the course of the global system, leading to compulsive consumerism, merciless environmental destruction, frantic accumulation of wealth, and exacerbated selfishness, all of which causes us to ignore those who have lagged behind and the indigent, who constitute this world's majority. In the chapters that make up the First Part, a socio economic machinery of imperfect functioning leading towards an imbalanced course that affects the planet as a whole is analyzed. This faces us with the two-fold effort of adjusting the course and, at the same time, improving the effectiveness of our way of functioning. We have taken it upon ourselves to understand what caused the crisis, the dynamics that originated it, and the circumstances that converged to make it explode with the virulence and global reach that it did. It is an essential analytical task to understand what happened and be able to evaluate the relevance and possible efficacy of the proposed solutions. If we do not have our own perspective, we will have to rely on the hegemonic vision, ineffective as the crisis itself showed yet repeated a thousand times by mainstream engines of strategic thought. From our viewpoint, this global crisis is not only financial even though it was, without doubt, triggered by the failures of the financial system. There are other reasons, other circumstances and other factors that generated the dynamics that led to the crisis. Without adjusting this dynamics, we run the serious risk of reproducing another cycle of crisis exit, recovery, growth, and return to another crisis.

To move towards sustainable development, not only it is possible but also necessary to overcome the great imbalances between and within countries. We need to construct a socially and environmentally responsible trajectory of organic growth; build new institutions that will allocate the available financial resources to serve production; abate inequality and poverty, not only for ethical motivations, but also because it becomes a necessary condition to ensure a dynamic balance between supply and demand. A better course and a more effective way of functioning does not precede the redistribution of opportunities, it stems from it.

Chapters that make up the Second Part, center on strategic aspects worth considering when designing solutions out of the crisis. They are useful references when assessing not only those elements included in the strategies to get out of the crisis, but also all other essential issues that may have been ignored or overlooked.

The course and systemic way of functioning are the focus of what is now being discussed or should be discussed at the political and economic levels. Each specific measure is important, but the directionality that the set of specific measures establishes is even more important. Strategic thought, policy orientations, and specific measures form part of a single challenge that is expressed on different levels. It is on this matter that we now focus our attention.

Part One

**INTERNATIONAL CRISIS:
ADJUSTING THE COURSE AND IMPROVING
THE SYSTEMIC FUNCTIONING**

CHAPTER I

Structural and functional roots of the crisis

The social, economic and political structure of a country conditions the way it functions, and the way a country functions impacts on its structure. Some structural factors produce serious functional imbalances, and dysfunctional ways of functioning contribute their impact to unleash explosive situations such as the present global crisis. On the face of this situation, it is necessary to choose among different options: from working on organic solutions that may ensure systemic sustainability to resorting to substitutes that help gain time but procrastinate outcomes. How do we characterize these options and what kind of measures are taken in each case? Is it possible to draw a path between self-regulation and excessive state intervention?

The social, economic and political structure of a country conditions the way it functions, and the way a country functions impacts on its structure. A deficient structure compromises the way it functions in terms of its direction and systemic performance, and the type of social and economic functioning produces direct effects on the very structure. This interrelation weaves the social, economic and political dynamics of a country. Something similar, though with greater institutional complexity, happens at the international level.

To exemplify how this structural-functional interrelation occurs let us take one of the most typical features among countries: inequality. In economic terms inequality implies that there are sectors of the population that are wealthier than others. In some cases the differences among sectors is abysmal and tends to grow bigger, while in others those differences are somewhat lesser but also tend to persist, or worsen.

Wealth differences in an unequal social and economic structure are expressed in many different ways, such as the segmentation of effective demand and the concentration of saving capacity.

EFFECTS RESULTING FROM THE SEGMENTATION
OF EFFECTIVE DEMAND

Effective demand segmentation causes affluent, conspicuous consumption sectors to coexist with popular sectors that can hardly meet their bare necessities; in between there are middle class sectors that consume basic goods and, whenever they have any surplus, reproduce at their own level the prevailing superfluous consumption pattern.

How does this demand segmentation impact upon the way of functioning? In several ways; some are of an economic nature, others of a social and political one. To begin with, superfluous consumption by affluent sectors and other middle class sectors generates a segment within the productive apparatus dedicated to producing superfluous goods. This results in a somewhat socially sub-optimal allocation of available resources and, at the same time, makes room for the emergence of economic players (superfluous goods suppliers) interested in sustaining this type of conspicuous consumption and the unequal structure that originates and underpins it.

There are more effects, however. Conspicuous consumption by affluent sectors is not capable of demanding all the goods and services generated by the productive apparatus, which unceasingly seeks to expand. To be able to sustain its growth, supply needs to be accompanied by a demand that is capable of keeping up with it. When the accumulation process becomes ever more concentrated, this balance is upset and, if there were not an intervention exogenous to the economic system, demand would be likely to lag behind.

DIFFERENT POSSIBLE REACTIONS
TO ADDRESS THE IMBALANCE

Here, a critical aspect of economic functionality takes the stage: *how the system reacts in order to adjust an imbalance that may jeopardize its expansion.* One formula –that is part of an organic growth– would consist in gradually raising consumers' income so that they may absorb with their own genuine resources the supply generated by the productive apparatus. If this formula works, supply and demand will accompany each other, even if they change their composition due to modifications in consumer preferences, which are strongly influenced by technological development, the launch of new goods and services, and a greater growth or appreciation of different sorts of satisfiers. Yet, regardless of this significant internal dynamics driven by innovation and discoveries, in aggregate terms, supply and demand, demand and supply, would grow organically.

If, however, there exists, as it occurs in reality, a process of wealth concentration that is projected into a concentration of income and, hence, into an unequal purchasing and saving power, then this organic growth will be jeopardized. A perilous gap would be opening between production and consumption capacity which, if not corrected, might block economic functioning and, ultimately, cause it to slide towards collapse: due to the lack of demand, businesses close down, unemployment grows, income falls, demand shrinks all the more, and what once had been a virtuous circle becomes a vicious descending spiral.

But will this be inevitably so? *No way. Before collapsing, the economic system strives to find other ways out, some of them healthy from a systemic viewpoint, while others only procrastinate the traumatic outcome.*

When tension appears due to a demand that is not capable of accompanying supply, we may resort to a battery of effective measures. These measures are intended to generate or gain access to resources that are capable of sustaining genuine demand. What are those resources?

(I)   Possibilities offered by the foreign sector

On option is to look at niches of foreign demand for our products. That is, a country may export to other countries a portion of the production that its domestic market is unable to absorb. Yet, this has a twofold limitation: on the one hand, many other countries compete to attract those same buyers, and hence, even though there are very interesting niches worth exploring, the key effort consists in becoming ever more competitive by enhancing productivity and positioning as far ahead as possible in terms of innovation and latest trends. There will be some exportable products over which the country has competitive advantages that will enable it not to depend solely on its domestic market. In those cases, it will remain to be seen who manages to export and how the revenue thus generated permeates into the country.

But beware: our production units are also receiving foreign competition in their own domestic market as we import goods and services that capture a portion of the resources generated within the country. This means that, on the foreign sector side, there are opportunities but also challenges that may turn into threats. A lot, a little, or nothing may be obtained from the foreign sector depending on the international circumstances and the efficacy of our own decisions.

(II) Possibility to generate genuine domestic resources

Another possibility is to generate within the country genuine income to fuel domestic consumption. There is a good policy space to ensure that the income the concentration process places in few hands gets distributed more equitably, eliminating or reducing inequity. On the one hand, at the macro-policies level, fiscal policy, public spending, prices and monetary stability, channeling of saving toward investments in the real economy and export promotion, weigh heavily. Well designed and better implemented these policies can re-distribute incomes making up for the prevailing accumulation process.

At the level of meso-economic initiatives there exists a huge margin for leading firms to strengthen their value chains, ensuring a fair distribution of results among those who are a part of it, and optimizing the secondary effects of their strategic decisions on other players.

Regarding a direct support to the bottom of the social and productive pyramid there are a number of modalities to channel knowledge of excellence, finance capital formation, assist in management development, devise good business structures, and facilitate market access.

As they are central to the book, these themes will be further addressed in other chapters.

(III) Decision to resort to substitute solutions

Now, what happens if due to political reasons, powerful interests, negligence or any other reason, those measures meant to generate a genuine income base are not actually implemented (or are implemented at a level bordering on insignificant or inconsequential cosmetics)? Well, as the system is not going to choose to commit suicide, it will resort to poor substitutes that do not solve but procrastinate on the issue of structural supply-demand imbalance. There are certain solutions based in repression and the imposition of authoritarian regimes, which we will not dwell on because we intend to focus on countries with more or less democratic systems (much could be said about just political democracy and full democracy which secures economic, social and environmental rights).

One of those substitute solutions is to fund families lacking genuine income so that they can turn into consumers. To this end credit allocation criteria are relaxed so that more people may gain access to loans that are renewed year after year. If the genuine income base of consumers has not improved after some credit cycles, they will fall into the typical, well-known situation of over-indebtedness. Purely and simply, this means that they are unable to meet their debts. When only a few fall into insolvency the problem may be contained, but when the phenomenon gains massive magnitude, the debacle is inevitable, as was the case with the infamous sub-prime mortgages and the explosive credit card segment. The consequences are plain to see.

EFFECTS RESULTING FROM SAVING CONCENTRATION

Unfortunately, the effects described above are not the only ones resulting from a social and economic structure characterized by the concentration of wealth. Saving concentration adds other set of specific effects.

The sectors that benefited from the concentration process accumulate huge financial surpluses that need to be recycled. In normal times, those surpluses are sought to be placed in financial investments or the real economy rather than remain immobilized, in order to –given certain risk levels– obtain the greatest possible yield*. However, as the concentration process restricts effective demand, there are fewer opportunities for good

---

* Even though a promising current of responsible investment is beginning to take significance, the yield and risk levels criteria to apply resources do not generally take into account the social and environmental impact of the investment, evidencing that there does not yet exist a self-regulatory mechanism capable of ensuring the best global use of available resources.

investments in the real economy, inducing the shifting of placements toward speculative financial transactions, including those oriented to sustaining consumption beyond the harsh limits of genuine income.

The financial system creates sophisticated products to absorb surpluses in need of recycling, obtaining high returns in the process. To lure surplus resources financial operators compete in terms of prices (rates of return) that are weighted against the risk inherent to each transaction. The greatest returns are obtained through bold financial engineering schemes and a certain concealment of the underlying risks, as was the case with the above mentioned sub-prime mortgages and credit cards, where responsibilities were diluted through complex operations with diverse intermediation and derivation chains. And thus emerge another factor that complements and reinforces the harmful vicious circle that leads to the crisis.

A CONCLUSION OPEN TO CHOICES

In closing, this analysis zeroed in on one of the key contemporary structural characteristics (inequality generated by a concentrating accumulation process) we may draw some important conclusions. Even though main conditions for a crisis to occur are derived from a concentrated social and economic structure, the resulting imbalances might be lessened without affecting the composition of that structure (and in some cases, they might even be solved), if the measures adopted as to the functional aspects offset the structural effects.

What is clear is that if on top of a vicious concentration structure a way of functioning unable to offset the destabilizing effects is added, crises such as the one almost the whole world is going through will become inevitable.

At this point of the analysis, the obvious is worth explaining. In spite of its critical importance, inequality is not the only factor impacting on the course of events. There are other very significant ones, and ignoring them would be a serious mistake since, in a way or another, they condition and fuel one another. Among others we can mentioned environmental deterioration, competitiveness, political regimes, global governance, military power asymmetries, media concentration, the threatening action of aggravated criminal systems, social values context and the influence our individual attitude has upon local processes and, indirectly, on the course of world events.

All these variables being at stake, some believe that their long or mid-term management is impracticable, while others think the opposite. As far as I am concerned, I observe that there exist self-regulatory systemic mechanisms to address the small or mid-sized imbalances produced by certain structural-functional combinations, but everything seems to indicate that the major imbalances exceed the self-regulatory capacity. While the economic system might endogenously adjust multiple small deviations, it is hard to deny that economy-exogenous decisions are required to overcome severe dysfunctionalities and ensure a smooth systemic functioning. The automatic pilot is good for certain legs of the journey, but when at critical or turbulent times strategic changes are required, we need to resort to our leadership to adjust and then sustain the course.

How leadership should be exercised, how critical strategic decisions should be addressed effectively is a complex endeavor requiring knowledge, experience, temper, a proper correlation of social forces and attachment to certain values that define our humanity. This is certainly an open socio-political issue, as at the individual level are the options we need to address in each life circumstance.

CHAPTER II

Not only Power but also a Better Course is needed

Well into the 21ˢᵗ century, we have not yet been able to face crucial contemporary challenges head-on. Old and new problems might be worked out by changing the course and reorienting wills and resources. It might seem ever less possible that we may, with "a little more of the same" or on automatic pilot, be able to overcome very difficult situations. The crucial challenge lies in preserving the ship and choosing a better course that may constructively admit such diverse interests and needs.

True, not only is vigor needed in the economy, in politics, in science and technology, in social movements, in our personal development, but also wisdom, intelligence, experience, ability, generosity to better use that power by choosing promising courses for everyone.

Well into the 21st century, and in spite of the vigorous economic growth, the phenomenal technology available, the enormous scientific knowledge, the unyielding effort by good-willed people, we have not yet been able to face crucial contemporary challenges head-on, or prevent affronts, destruction, distress and insecurity from pullulating. Definitely, it is not just a matter of adding more power to our engines but also of re-routing the course.

New problems appear and old problems are reproduced which might be worked out by changing the course and reorienting wills and resources. Poverty, inequality, fierce antagonisms, famines, severe environmental deterioration, the explosion of oil and food prices, increased aggravated crime systems, financial crises in central markets with global implications, add challenges (and these are not the only ones) that are very difficult to face. Some say that these types of problems have always existed, and they will be worked out as a result of the "normal" evolution of things. Let us hope they are right for the sake of the planet and of those who inhabit it, although in fact there is evidence to the contrary that does not cease to accumulate.

When tensions mount to the point of jeopardizing the fate of immense majorities, when conflicts and confusion no longer affect only some sectors or regions but threaten the systemic functioning, it becomes very difficult to continue to believe that it is possible to overcome situations with "a little more of the same", or that some enlightened being or automatic pilot will be able to solve problems, obtain better answers and clear dark clouds per se. Rather, there is a need for each of us to assume a greater share of responsibility and determination to face those challenges: easy to say, not so easy to assume.

Changing does not mean dismissing the past indiscriminately; the efforts made, the accomplishments, experiences, count a lot. Changing requires using history, what has been learned, what has already been conquered, as well as sorrows, mistakes and regressions, in order to be able to advance in better condition. Adjusting the course has nothing to do with burning our precious ship; instead, it implies rerouting it towards a better port with greater social cohesion and environmental preservation.

When we wonder what each one of us can do to adjust the systemic course, thousands of doubts spring as we compare the complexity of the challenge with our modest strengths. It is worth the while to acknowledge the magnitude of the purpose, and that there exist contextual parameters conditioning any action; also that the history of civilizations teaches that individuals and organizations impact upon the course that social, economic and political processes take. Even though nobody per se and in isolation is capable of generating systemic changes, the mobilization of the whole generates the conditions for that transformation to materialize. We need to review behaviors and clearly express where we mean to head for. Each opinion counts, each mobilized will make a difference, regardless of the existence of a diversity of visions and preferences in relation to the new courses. This plurality of viewpoints and interests make it possible to enrich the construction with everyone's contribution.

VOICES AND INTERESTS

In fact, multiple players are involved, each one of them holding and exercising very different shares of power. Not all voices are equally heard; some of them echo in many corners of the planet, while others only resound in the family circle or the neighborhood. Yet, the development attained in the field of communications makes it possible for thoughts, proposals, longings, to circulate more than in the past, and be known even in very remote corners of countries and the planet. In spite of the strong concentration verified in the media, a large diversity of small and medium-sized engines that generate content find alternative channels to spread new ideas, experiences, proposals, calls for action, surmounting conventional hurdles and wire fences.

In the marching of society, almost without exception, each one is loaded with interests and needs (of material, psychological and spiritual nature) that would like to be able to meet. Those individual interests and needs may help, facilitate or impede the realization of the other ones. To release energies that may reinforce our capacity to do, it is then necessary to de-antagonize to the greatest possible extent such accumulation of interests and needs. Yet, to reinforce our capacity to be, as individuals and as a planet, it is at the same time necessary to align those same interests with a different perspective on welfare, as well as not only a short-term, but also a mid and long-term horizon.

De-antagonizing implies facing and working out-rather than hiding-differences; employing all the intelligence and generosity we are able to gather to find creative ways that may help attain acceptable degrees of satisfaction for the different interests and needs. Intelligence is necessary to design solutions that may help reach convergence and reward knowledge, innovation and work; generosity is necessary to secure spaces for those that have been left behind.

Another notion of welfare would facilitate more existentially meaningful searches rather than getting us stuck in an exacerbated and alienated consumerism that is maintained on the basis of promoting permanent dissatisfaction, envy, and anxiety. That new aspiration profile would help reorient ourselves towards building societies where peace, security, good-neighborliness, cooperation, weigh more than a strenuous and selfish "save himself who can".

In the economic arena, there exist functional mechanisms in imperfect markets whereby resources and energies are allocated among multiple possible choices. These mechanisms enable the interaction of millions of wills of different natures and sizes. Since each will is the bearer of its own sector or individual interests and needs, the rationality of the whole emerges from massive economic forces funneled through their two-fold role, as they are supply and demand at the same time. It is impossible to ignore the dynamism of these mechanisms, although it is critical to assess the consequences of the different degrees of imperfection in our markets and the way they work today, which is not the only possible one. That is, assessing where we are headed for, at what social and personal cost and how effectively we are doing so, what problems we solve and what problems we generate as we move forward, who benefit a lot and who benefit less, who are harmed to a certain extent and who, instead, do not manage to survive, and succumb.

Our engines are not short of power; the crucial challenge lies in the course and how to manage, with a new direction, to constructively align such diverse interests and needs. The actual complexity of the challenge becomes all the more evident when we realize that we must make decisions based on always incomplete information, pressed and biased due to the struggles for interests and needs we are a part of. Caught inside that fog, we can only resort to a mix of knowledge, experience and intuition, equipped with an ethical compass having compassion, generosity and everyone's dignity as its north.

Who are the leading and the supporting actors in that search for new courses?

CHAPTER III

Facing the crisis: stampedes and solutions

In a crisis, individuals either strive to avoid its effects or pass them on to others. As in any stampede, he or she who does not manage to move to the side in time ends up being run over by the herd. How can we face this crisis in such a way as to mitigate its effects and come out of it in the best possible shape? This will depend on how the contextual circumstances (that we do not control) evolve, but also –and very specially– on the way we ourselves react: old problems persist that have undermined our potentiality, and new decisions need to be made. This does fall within the orbit of our responsibility.

We are faced with a world crisis triggered by the mishap in the financial systems of central countries. Its effects are being felt everywhere, though in different ways. There is a pervasive economic slowdown and, in many cases, stagnation or recession. The major international players are analyzing defense lines and exit strategies; they may have a bearing on the course of events but cannot avoid them. They seek to coordinate their policies in such a way as to contain the first reaction, which was "every man for himself" or, more precisely, me for myself at the others' expense. It remains to be seen whether such coordination can be sustained, and how emerging economies will react, particularly, emerging economic drivers such as China, India, Brazil and Mexico.

In a crisis, each one strives to avoid its effects or pass them on to others. As in any stampede, he who does not manage to move to the side in time ends up being run over by the herd. Those who are best positioned use their greater economic power, and their better access to information, contacts, and knowledge, to protect their interests more effectively. Some do that within the confines of legality and others outside it. The majority knows that rather than helping the least empowered, individually forsaking each one's own interest facilitates the predatory action of ravens and wolves; hence the importance of coming up with answers at the policy and regulatory level.

As time goes by, lessons appear that those well-advised actors, as well as fishers in troubled waters, are able to internalize. The rest, who are the majority, do not manage to unravel the logic of the crisis, take the blows, return to the herd of the gullible, and fall again in a consumerism that strips their days of any meaning. Ravens and wolves change their robes, purify their lineage, and give way to a new brood of unscrupulous climbers.

How can we face this crisis in such a way as to mitigate its effects and come out of it in the best possible shape? This will depend on how the contextual circumstances (that we do not control) evolve, but also –and very specially– in the way we ourselves react: old problems persist that have undermined our potentiality, and new decisions wait to be made. This does fall within the orbit of our responsibility.

COMING TOGETHER

In my opinion, the most critical factor in facing the crisis is not economic but political and social: we need to join forces, to get together in order to tackle the challenges and work on the new opportunities successfully. We have worn ourselves out for too long with internal struggles, with antagonisms that drain energy and affect our agility to react. It makes no sense to demonize the opponent and address the other from the only truth that, of course, is our own. Political cannibalism does not enrich society; it impoverishes it. We must stop this; mean-spirited actions are already an unbearable dead weight. Our piece of land will never be an orchard in the middle of the dessert; as we erode our neighbour's farm, we fall together with him.

A unifying leadership is needed, one that is adroit enough to align interests and needs. He who does not know how, does not want or is unable to do it, should be punished at the ballot box. There is no more room for the all-or-nothing attitude; compromises are required in order to establish short and mid-term agreements that are transparent, trick-free, and contain safeguards to preserve goals in case course deviations occur should circumstances change. Frankness is expected, and a fair allocation of results is sought, without resorting to any form of cronyism or patronage. Political intermediation is useful to the extent that their interests as brokers do not affect the interests of the population as a whole. Cahoots aimed to behead some in order to give way to others are not good either; as though the replacement of individuals instead of ways of acting could work the miracle. Some politicians want to convince us that if their faction got to rule, things would be very different; but we have grown tired of realizing that mere face changes do not solve our problems.

We have the leaders we have, and with them –or in spite of them– we will have to move forward. In politics you cannot improvise, and ousting or neutralizing governments is a drawback, rather than a contribution. In point of fact, it is preferable to come up with a suboptimal but positive solution that may be implemented immediately, than with an eventually superior but uncertain one in terms of whether it will be ultimately likely to be implemented. Instead of the eternal attempt at neutralizing governments led by rivals, the focus should be placed on aligning transparent interests, needs, and values, using the whole range of modalities to build sustainable multi-partisan agreements. Later on, there will be time to evaluate who really made sincere efforts for us to come together and create solutions, and who, instead, concentrated on imposing their mean-spirited siren songs and false images.

TRAVELING DOWN ONE'S OWN PATH

The prevailing structures weaken with the crisis, and this might be beneficial. The lava melts foundations and we would be right not to rebuild that which provoked the destruction. Opportunities to develop solutions that are appropriate to our circumstances open up, instead of replicating formulae that were designed for other realities. With prudence and creativity, we can start building our own trajectory of sustainable development.

The homogenization of strategic thinking was disastrous for the countries of the South; it led us to import visions, agendas, solutions that do not correlate with our interests and uniqueness; it reduced the range of options and mutilated our creativity. It is imperative for us to fully recover the capacity to think and innovate. Those think tanks, those engines of analyses, assessments, recommendations –enshrined by strong interest groups– are merely one of various possible perspectives; they have the right to remain contributing their share but in no way to presume that they do so from "the truth". Their points of view must be filtered by those of our analysts, thinkers, scientists, philosophers, spiritual leaders. This does not mean to turn our back on the world and return to the parochial, but rather to trust in our criteria more so that external opinions enrich, and not substitute, our interpretation and decision-making process.

This is even more pressing in the context of contemporary acceleration (1), where setting the course takes pre-eminence over the mere generation of power, when we need to design early alerts to detect deviations and unwanted effects, adopt more effective regulatory mechanisms, and choose leaders who are well experienced at steering at the pace required to accompany the rapid changes in circumstances.

ADJUSTING THE STRUCTURE AND THE WAY OF FUNCTIONING

The new course calls for a better distribution of efforts and their results. It is necessary to promote a self-sustainable virtuous dynamic: starting by adjusting our own way of functioning so as to generate transformations in the social and economic structure that may favor, in turn, a permanent improvement in the systemic functioning.

When we talk about adjusting the way in which we function, we mean taking measures and adopting policies with macro-impact, not just merely proposing special, high-profile but hardly significant programs. There is no room for the political cosmetics of changing something so that nothing changes. Even though there still are gullible individuals who can be deceived, the very social and economic dynamics ends up being inexorable; the crisis speaks for itself.

The direction taken is a cornerstone of the development process when chosen with wisdom and the aid of a good ethical compass. A course agreed upon by consensus combines interests, needs, and values in time; if well conceived, it is a convergence and driving factor for the conglomerate of forces that make up a society. Other cornerstones are knowledge (based on education, on scientific and technological research, on fostering innovation and creativity) and entrepreneurial capacity, which should be advocated as one of the most treasured social assets. Being involved in the development of these cornerstones is a responsibility, not a source of privileges.

WHERE TO START FROM

To address the effects of the crisis there are quick impact measures that, while improving our way of functioning, may strengthen our economic and social structure. They not only boost recovery but are also capable of reorienting without halting our productive process.

It is necessary to be on the alert, because every time a crisis occurs the siren songs urge us to relapse on what is already known, as though there were no time or space for new solutions capable of containing the negative effects of transforming us. Today's reality brings along the good and the not-so-good; it is as valuable as experience. But it will be necessary to separate the wheat from the chaff and give way to better structures that may guarantee the chosen course.

In essence, it is a matter of mobilizing our full realization capacity; taking advantage of our entire productive potential, both the active one and the one that up to today has been immobilized. It is indispensable that the bottom of the social and productive pyramid be mobilized through the adoption of macro-economic measures, meso-economic initiatives, and direct-support actions such as, among others, inclusive business developers, socially and environmentally responsible investor networks, and small production investment funds; all within the strategic context of boosting productive chains in order to maximize value added, develop regional economies and prioritize education, science and technology.

INEQUALITY AND CRITICAL INCOME DISTRIBUTION

Much is being said about the financial origin of the crisis, and quite less about the array of other structural reasons that made the implosion possible. One of the most important ones is the growing concentration of income taking place within each economy as well as at the level of the international economic system as a whole. Income concentration generates markets oversaturated with conspicuous consumption next to impoverished markets unable to meet their basic needs. In contexts where the supply of goods and services does not cease to grow and the strongly concentrated demand cannot accompany such growth in supply, serious bottlenecks occur. To be able to continue functioning without introducing changes, the economic system responds with short-term pump-fuelling solutions: on the one hand, it strives to expand demand by causing debtors to over-borrow rather than providing them with better income (an intrinsic contradiction of the concentration process); on the other hand, it seeks to recycle resources from surplus sectors by channeling them into financial placements that are ever more dissociated from a real economy that is unable to grow organically as a result of the concentration process. The financial system leads this game from which it draws juicy results. Yet, at the same time, it gets stuck there as it makes it possible for consumers who are not income-backed to over-borrow, and recycles surpluses resulting from the concentration process into speculative placements.

Even when this is a critical dimension, we must be aware of the fact that by merely finding a solution to the increasing concentration of wealth and income, we would not manage to untie all the knots that block our development; in fact, there are other crucial variables, such as environmental preservation, technological and productivity development, entrepreneurial spirit, management efficiency, communities' social capital, that all strongly impact the course of events; ignoring them also brings about systemic imbalances. It is, however, undeniable that inequality has acquired such magnitude worldwide that today it is one of the major threats to the viability of present development. The income distribution "factor" is thus not only associated with the values of justice and respect for the human condition but also to the very stability and sustainability of our functioning as a nation. Abating the concentration process, and its consequences in terms of inequality and poverty, becomes not just a necessary but also an indispensable, though not sufficient, condition to improve the social and economic structure and secure a better systemic functioning.

In the best style of former president Bill Clinton, today the message offered to those who navigate the superficiality of processes might be "it is the concentration process, stupid".

CHAPTER IV

Pettiness and Dignity in the Face of the Crisis

In a crisis, not just each one's temperament, resilience, and capacity to overcome adversity is put to the test, but also our values, gregarious spirit and solidarity with others. There is a majority who loses and a minority who wins; some react mean-spiritedly; others, with dignity. When the water lowers you can see who is who; where there is rock and where only mud. Reality is the way it is and should not intimidate us; we would rather see how to mobilize valuable intangible assets that are capable of generating a huge energy, among others, our capacity to take initiative, to organize new institutions, to generate synergies, to add efforts. Siren songs cause confusion and deviate the course toward consumerist alienation, value nihilism, and substitute happiness. The price paid is huge.

In a crisis, not only each one's temperament, resilience, capacity to overcome adversity is put to the test, but also our values, gregarious spirit and solidarity with others. With the crisis, there is a majority who loses and a minority who wins because it can and knows how to take advantage of the circumstances that the very crisis generates. Among the ones who lose prevail both middle-income and poor sectors, even though not all suffer equally. Indigence, malnutrition, overcrowding and insecurity rise; networks of social protection and schooling drop. There appears the "new poor, "or middle-income sectors who slide toward scarcity. Large majorities feel ignored and punished by a society that is annoyed and frightened.

In the face of this, how do the sectors least affected by the crisis react? Some mean-spiritedly; others with dignity. There are those who profit from the crisis at the expense of other people's pain; there are also those who only struggle for their own salvation, trampling whoever they need to trample in order to come out unhurt; others protect what is theirs, but also try to help those who have been most affected; even in the crisis they endeavor for fair development.

Those who profit from other people's pain, unremorsefully take advantage of the weakness of others to appropriate their assets or obtain greater results. Pettiness is with them, and those who have been affected are mere preys. Helping is not in their nature; from their ethical perspective, why would they do it?

There are well-off individuals who, in times of bonanza, develop philanthropic actions, but when faced with a crisis cut their contributions to social projects or just causes, which become their first adjustment variable. Thus they evidence the little value they attach to these causes, as well as the fragile loyalty they profess to them, which, in times of abundance, they bragged about supporting. What hurts, is that in spite of the crisis, their standard of living does not change drastically but only marginally; they adjust their expenses but their recreational activities, their travels, second residences, memberships, superfluous consumption, do not disappear.

The sectors worst affected by crises survive the storm as best they possibly can; the circumstances of scarcity and abandonment harden. There are those who only see ways out in crime and addictions, but many others strengthen ties, reinforce solidarity in the face of uneasiness. Creativity sharpens, though on the basis of improvisation, of trial and error. Amidst the precariousness of resources, talent and determination emerge; yet, due to the lack of effective support systems, they have limited access to knowledge, to modern business engineering, to timely information, to empowering contacts. Though very worthy, achievements and results end up being meager.

In a crisis, the water lowers and you can see the bottom of the river; determine who is who; where there is rock and where only mud. It is touching to recognize in that hurricane of fears and selfishness, of confusion and acceleration, those who fight not only for themselves; people from different walks of life and experience who struggle for what is theirs and others'. They radiate dignity, mobilize hope; also showing the extent of the absurd and immense sterilization of efforts that our course and way of functioning bring about.

In the face of the crisis, maybe the most urgent and peremptory challenge consists in being able to stand tall above disagreements. Indeed, we need to take initiative by helping one another, work to achieve convergence, mobilize and share knowledge, adjust the course, organize action, improve the way of functioning. The fronts are diverse and hard to tackle if we are divided.

Reality is the way it is, and should not intimidate us; there is much to know and recognize. We confine to a pitiful secondary role valuable intangible assets such as our capacity to take initiative, to organize new institutions, to generate synergies, and to add rather than withdraw efforts. It is from there that a tremendous, poorly-used, energy emanates. To deploy it, we need to reflect, come together in an organized manner, exercise our free will appropriately, and stay away from paralyzing determinism as well as risky voluntarism.

Each society, each generation, chooses paths and modalities to tackle what it considers obstacles to its development. There are times when the heap of problems seems immense and no ways out can be seen: the man in the street and even many leaders feel overwhelmed, unable to face their circumstances. Siren songs cause confusion and deviate the course toward consumerist alienation, value nihilism, and substitute happiness. The price paid is huge.

Faced with this, there is no choice but to meet head-on the challenges, which are as many and diverse as the circumstances each individual, each social group, each country, the entire planet, are confronted with. It is in that diversity of perspectives we must act, enriching ourselves with what each one can contribute, having one eye on the course and the other one on a permanent improvement of our way of functioning. There is where we need to focus, working with or without a crisis; working to understand what happens; working to establish a directionality; working to align interests, needs and emotions; working to mobilize wills; working to organize action with efficacy. With that effort, with that critical work that is both collective and individual, we can aspire to come closer to one of the most heartfelt contemporary utopias: ensuring sustainability, peace and justice for our development as a society and a higher sense of purpose to our personal existential development.

CHAPTER V

Leading in the Vertigo of Contemporary Acceleration

As a result of a combination of social, technological and environmental forces, the world faces a stage of vertiginous acceleration that exceeds the thresholds of contention that were known so far. The speed of change makes complex economic processes difficult to manage, leaving countries exposed to harsh episodes of systemic recklessness with very serious and destructive consequences. Which changes are necessary to address?

As a result of a combination of social, technological, and environmental forces, the world faces a stage of vertiginous acceleration that exceeds the thresholds of contention that were known so far. The speed of change[*] makes the complex economic processes difficult to manage, leaving countries exposed to harsh episodes of systemic recklessness with very serious and destructive consequences.

This situation requires addressing drastic changes in the way of operating, the following among others:

I.   In periods of acceleration it is necessary, more than ever, to focus on the systemic course so we can reach where we are headed much faster while piling up desired and undesired effects; the latter with the possibility of being dramatically traumatic; the imperative is to ensure the direction since power is not something that is missing. Having a course implies making explicit the type of system that is desired, the results

---

* I thank Marcelo de Santis for inspiring the writing of this chapter.

that are being pursued and expected, how they are meant to be obtained including their environmental impact and how results will be distributed among countries and social sectors.

II. In order to avoid and not only mitigate incidents of systemic recklessness, it is a must to establish more effective mechanisms of process regulation, a critical yet also controversial aspect as it is difficult to determine the right dose of intervention with accuracy: too little regulation makes frantic behavior possible and too much may stifle our initiative. iii. It will also be necessary to design early alarm mechanisms in order to detect sidetracks or undesired effects; the typical alarms, those that perceive the outburst of an event once it takes place, are not sufficient because in contexts of acceleration they do not allow us to react in time and act accordingly; we need alarms that go off when what will become fast events start being glimpsed.

IV. Not being a uniform or universal phenomenon, contemporary acceleration aggravates the processes of differentiation; it generates winners and losers among and within countries faster. In the current systemic circumstances new beneficiaries may emerge, yet in general there are many more harmed people that thicken the majorities that lag behind and deepen social and international disputes; as a consequence, coexistence, security, and even democratic governance are dramatically affected. Acceleration forces the adoption as a critical dimension of the new course of comprehensive strategies aimed to avoid reproducing, and even more so aggravating, inequality.

III. Contemporary acceleration leads to making decisions based on information that is generated along the way. Well or not so well, we make out what is familiar while the new events erupt challenging our comprehension. The sudden changes of circumstances shorten the time for reflection and demand quick pronouncements, increasing the possibility of erring, of acting at the wrong moment and of not perceiving the complexity of novel processes. We need to acquire new frameworks of analysis, various types of approaches free from ideological fundamentalisms, to be open to grasp the new phenomena, to anticipate their consequences and to propose a more diverse range of solutions tailored to the very different local situations.

Leading in these conditions requires to thoroughly understand these and other critical aspects of the new circumstances; to know how to adjust to contemporary speed and complexity; to count on teams that are qualified and experienced in facing unexpected situations; pilots with mettle that know how to lead in the frenzy of the acceleration and agilely react without overlooking the ethical compass that enables to maintain the course agreed upon beyond the needed short term maneuvers.

We still have to see if it is possible to lower contemporary acceleration. Maybe by adjusting the systemic course, speed would cede some more ground to quality of life; growing speeds leave their mark in people and organizations. Acceleration should lead us to take better care of the prized humanity; it is not a choice to sacrifice the environment, social justice, spiritual development. We need appropriate spaces to recover our rhythms and abilities, our creativity, our capacity to reflect, to contemplate; we need to disengage from acceleration's constant frenzy. Dawns, dusks, affections, relationships, enigmas can dazzle us way beyond rushes and desires.

If resisting contemporary speed and acceleration were some kind of mission impossible, then at stake would be how to channel them through new strategies for the benefit of the social ensemble, preserving the environment and enabling the full deployment of our human essence, closely linked to the never ending search of adding meaning and justice to our lives.

CHAPTER VI

Systemic faults in our way of functioning

The international crisis we are going through expresses serious systemic failures in the way central countries function. The very heart of the global system is failing and seeks protection in order not to be rolled over by the same forces it contributed to unleash. What happened compares to a financial tsunami created by the way in which we have decided to organize and function rather than by nature. Yet, there is no point in deceiving ourselves: there exist other structural causes in addition to the financial ones. Today the challenge lies in making the emergency measures facilitate the beginning of fundamental changes; bringing the systemic functioning back to exactly the same condition it was in before it short-circuited and crashed would be the worst of alternatives.

The international crisis we are going through expresses serious systemic failures in the way central countries function. The very heart of the global system is failing and seeks protection in order not to be rolled over by the same forces it contributed to unleash. What happened compares to a financial tsunami created by the way in which we have decided to organize and function rather than by nature. Yet, there is no point in deceiving ourselves: there exist other structural causes in addition to the financial ones.

We need to reflect upon, and review, certain concepts, even the most widely accepted ones, acknowledge the reality of the processes underway, and depart from dogmatic predicaments. It is time to review the "global contract" in depth, recognizing its underlying rationale and the unforeseen effects caused by the way it works. Even when there is much to transform and adjust, there also exist assets that are worth preserving; swinging from one end to the other of the pendulum will be of no use.

In order to fully understand what has happened, it is necessary to take into account the unwanted externalities of the current international economic system; to acknowledge how they have been generated, to consider how to abate them and to avoid their possible reproduction. Unwanted externalities are present in the systemic crisis and also in the eventual transition into a better systemic functioning; they will condition the new agreements necessary to redesign the financial architecture and reorient the real economy.

THE FINANCIAL LEG OF THE CRISIS

It might seem that the crisis has a financial origin and if the financial system was reformed, the crisis would reverse until finally disappearing. This is a half-truth. It is a fact that the financial system has run wild; it dangerously departed from the real economy to the extent that it thought it was the engine and pilot of the global economy. The movement of financial flows acquired a phenomenal magnitude. In real time, a computer click mobilizes entire seas of resources from one point to another of the globe. Financial dealers, who originally had one eye on their financial dealings and the other one on the real economy, later placed their two eyes, ears, nose, and intuition on just reaping revenue from their ever more sophisticated financial moves. Thus, financial spaces grew apart from their anchors in the real economy. Greed and doing things the easy way, earning a thousandth that multiplied by billions created instant fortunes, added to the factors heading the process towards the abyss.

Regulators, for their part, did not know how or did not want to, fulfill their control and required role of alerting; the prevailing belief was that the market could self-regulate and, if it happened to run out of control, corrective mechanisms would appear endogenously. But the market ran amok and corrective mechanisms only appeared at the hand of the political authority and at huge systemic costs.

The unbridled financial system happens to be one of the structural causes of the crisis; yet its genesis and implosion are associated with another critical structural characteristic of the way in which markets work: the extended processes of income and wealth concentration, both among countries and within each country.

THAT UNDERESTIMATED WEALTH CONCENTRATION PROCESS

I. Wealth concentration among countries

The abysmal economic differences existing among countries generate all sorts of antagonisms, conflicts endured by those who compete at a disadvantageous position, impositions founded on imbalances of power, virulent reactions, repression, punishment, unwanted demographic flows, homogenization of ideas with an epicenter in the central countries which limits the capacity to appreciate differences and impoverishes responses.

The international wealth concentration process generates over-saturated markets of conspicuous consumption and impoverished markets with their population's basic needs insufficiently met. Between those poles there are intermediate countries with disparate living standards and consumer demand levels. When serious bottlenecks occur within central countries as a result of a production supply that does not cease to grow and, in order to sustain that growth, depends upon a demand that does not accompany such supply increase because it is strongly concentrated. As a result, the systemic functioning searches for circumstantial solutions that may allow it to move ahead with an intact structure. These types of solutions that facilitate access to consumption but not to income (which would involve affecting the distributional structure) require a financial system that pushes to the greatest extent possible the concentration process viability limits; it operates as an ephemeral ditch attempting to contain the effects stemming from the systemic way of functioning.

While this happens in central countries, some of the large emerging economies implement structural adjustments that may enable them to attain robust growth rates. Countries such as China, India, Brazil, and the dynamic South Asian countries occupy preponderant global positions, accumulating bulky trade and financial surpluses. In that situation, by deferring the adoption of systemic adjustments that might resolve their structural imbalances, the central economies run the risk of being unable to maintain their global leadership roles and affect the rest of the countries in the short or mid-term.

53

II.   Wealth concentration within countries

Within emerging economies, the inequities resulting from a concentration process are expressed in widespread poverty, precarious governance, a weak productive apparatus, frequent external bottlenecks, and a fragile domestic market; all these factors act by destabilizing the systemic functioning and generating recurrent functional and structural crises.

As it was mentioned above, central economies have more resources, and they are in a position to contain, for some time, the negative effects of economic concentration within their own economies; yet, if that process is not reverted, the effects ultimately find a way to express out themselves.

When there is sustained production growth and wealth gets concentrated, the economic logic causes structural imbalances to occur. What the productive apparatus produces is oriented, on the one hand, towards satisfying those sectors that benefit from such concentration. Yet, since such demand is insufficient to absorb supply in its totality, it also seeks to find markets in non-favoured sectors. The affluent consumer-oriented demand can only grow by fostering superfluous consumption; by contrast, the supply oriented to the rest of the population depends on the possibility of setting up mechanisms that may facilitate their consumption beyond their economic possibilities. The financial system, which is an essential part of the economic system, develops according to those circumstances and grows explosively on the basis of "solutions" it manages to contribute to that systemic functioning of a concentrating nature: it recycles surplus resources in financial placements and provides financing for a consumption that would not be able to be expressed in the market based on its own resources. It is painful but enlightening to trace the effects of the concentration process that filter like lava through the economic system until they ultimately lead to an explosive systemic crisis.

A HIGHLY DANGEROUS COMBINATION OF PHENOMENA

Superfluous consumption is one of the ways the affluent sectors have to allocate the resources that exceed the satisfaction of their basic needs. Yet they are not the only ones to fall in this type of consumption; the middle and low sectors –with access to financing– also participate. By means of aggressive advertising, the market tries to constantly expand the limits of which different social groups consider as basic needs, artificially generating an almost constant dissatisfaction that derives in consumption as it is cunningly intertwined with complex aspects of existential anxiety. The huge mass of conspicuous consumption results in perverse systemic effects as it supports a production level that is not consistent with the prevailing distributional structure (financial overheating resulting from over-indebtedness); besides, it leads a fair amount of the productive apparatus to produce those superfluous goods and services, consolidating a sub-optimal structure of allocation of resources and adding parties interested in supporting the concentration process.

Surplus resources in the sectors that benefited from the concentration process are placed in financial investments or the real economy, which, as they mature, reinforce such concentration. The application of resources follows yield and risk criteria; in other words, either directly or through intermediary institutions, they seek placements that may ensure the best possible return given a certain accepted level of risk. These yield-risk criteria are not generally associated with other criteria relating the investment's social and environmental impact, which evidences that there does not yet exist a systemic mechanism that is capable of ensuring a better global use of available savings*. Since each resource placement option competes with others, a struggle to attract those resources occurs. Part of that struggle is legitimate and based on taking advantage of innovations and being more efficient than the competition; but another part is illegitimate and sustained on maximizing returns on the basis of insider information, monopoly positions, profiting by corrupt means, criminal systems, exploited labor, environmental destruction, wars, etc. and hiding risks and responsibilities through complex intermediation and bypass operations and chains.

As mentioned above, the concentration process also generates a gap between the actual demand from middle and low-income population levels and the supply of goods and services oriented to them. The most systemically adequate approach to closing that structural gap would be to dismantle the concentration process and foster the development of genuine demand relying on its own resources. When this does not happen and the growth in the productive apparatus requires a demand counterpart that is not able to accompany it at a similar rate,

---

* A new current of investors –a significant yet minor one if we compare it against the astronomical contemporary financial movements– do weigh their investment choices on the basis of social and environmental criteria.

the conditions are created for the financial system to seek to expand such demand beyond its ability to pay. This situation and consumer over-borrowing are just one footstep away; the sub-prime mortgage bubble is perhaps the most dramatic but not the only example of this perverse process.

So the conjunction of a structural process of wealth concentration that reinforces itself, the subsequent expansion both of conspicuous consumption and of middle and low income consumer over-indebtedness, coupled with a segment of the financial system that –with sophisticated greed– artificially maintains the status quo beyond the severe limits imposed by the concentrating functioning, account for the rationale that leads to the crisis. Certainly, the specific trajectories leading to the crisis are mediated by historical and institutional circumstances that differ from one place to another.

THE EMERGENCY AND COMING OUT OF THE CRISIS

Time and again it is said that when your house is on fire the first thing you need to do is put out the fire. This is a tricky allegory as it suggests that in an emergency there is no choice but to fight the destructive fire in the best possible manner; later on we will have time to find out its origin and reconstruct whatever needs to be reconstructed. Yet, when such havoc is created on a system, the indispensable emergency actions should be designed jointly with quick functional adjustments to such system. Otherwise we would be running the risk that no sooner is one fire spot put out, others will appear at unexpected places and times. In sum, the point is that the necessary emergency measures should carry within themselves the germ of systemic adjustments.

The issue is that there is not just a single way to address a systemic emergency, and that the worst one of all would be that which is capable of bringing the systemic functioning back to exactly the same condition it was in before it short-circuited and crashed. In coming chapters, we will try to identify some of the characteristics of a way out of the crisis that might create the conditions for configuring a fairer and more effective systemic functioning.

CHAPTER VII

Crisis in the United States: Suggestions from the South

The crisis in the USA poses major domestic challenges. A virulent struggle is taking place among sectors to avoid or elude the costs of the present situation. While some profit from it, the rest try to subsist until the storm is weathered. The solutions adopted will strongly condition future trajectories. When the turbulence passes it will be very difficult to transform the newly established dynamics. In the face of that, a puzzled look will be of no use. It is critical that the consequences and implications of the different 'way out' strategies be considered in the light of the country's founding principles. The crisis does not require other principles; rather, it puts the existing ones to the test. The country needs to avoid costly bailouts that instead of re-situate it on a more inclusive base might reinforce concentration of wealth processes.

The United States is going through a crisis that is affecting the country and the rest of the world. Its causes are complex and diverse. Quite some time ago, Juan Eugenio Corradi offered his sharp vision on the nature of the process that originates the current crisis in Opinion Sur Geopolitical section (www.opinionsur.org.ar). Based on that perspective and on our own experience in the South, I wondered if I would have anything to contribute to American public opinion.

At the beginning this idea appeared to me somewhat odd because advice and suggestions more often tend to follow a course North-South rather than South-North. I also recalled the resistance with which we in the South received the canned solutions that were generated in certain organizations and think tanks of the North. I told myself that, out of respect for our brothers in the North, I did not have the right to reproduce those mistakes. Any suggestion I offer would not be as comprehensive or definitive to those who, living in the situation, have a better understanding of its potentials and difficulties. These circumstances are innumerable, unique, and change over time; sometimes they are obvious, other times they are deeply rooted in long-standing traditions, visions and national concerns. With that said, the following lines are simple suggestions offered to reflect upon what may or may not serve as an input to those who have taken the task of facing such a severe crisis.

THE NEED TO RESPECT BASIC PRINCIPLES WHEN SEARCHING FOR SOLUTIONS

Each society carries some basic principles that shape its identity and influence its behavior. These principles must be respected and integrated into any solution. Only if some of those principles were incompatible with the current times could they be abandoned or adjusted. My aim is not to list a set of US foundational principles that still guide citizen behavior. For the purpose of this article let me pick out only some of the principles that are most valued by the American people:

I. The principle of freedom of thought and of creation and management of all kinds of initiatives that do not go against the law.
II. The democratic principle of offering equal opportunities to all.
III. The principle of national unity and of care for the most vulnerable.
IV. The principle of responsibility for our acts and for the consequences derived from them.

There are certainly many other important principles but, as I have just pointed out, this set provides a good support for the suggestions that will be offered in the following lines.

CO-RESPONSIBILITY WHEN FACED WITH THE CRISIS AND THE SOLUTIONS

Although to different degrees, really all or almost all of us are responsible for a crisis. This is not the time to build –it is also very difficult to do so– a final and detailed scale of each one's degree of responsibility. Yet it is clear that there are great differences among the actors involved.

It could be stated that the direct responsibility lies in those who generated the speculative bubbles that have burst, plus in those who did not exercise the control that was their institutional duty. They are the ones that should face up to the major costs of way out of the crisis. Major responsibility also falls on those who designed the policies and regulations that led the country into this crisis.

There are other co-responsible actors who, without having produced those bubbles, participated in them and benefited from their existence. They should also assume their share of responsibility for the risks they took and for the subsequent results. To a certain extent, all the remaining sectors of American society –by action or omission– have decreasing degrees of responsibility and, as such, will have to shoulder –in that smaller proportion– the costs of the solutions.

Why this emphasis on the different degrees of co-responsibility? It happens that interests groups also operate in crises. The most agile, connected or informed will try as much as possible to pass on the costs derived from their co-responsibility on to other shoulders. In the midst of the turbulence and fear and of the confusion that grip the common minds in a crisis, the most seasoned take advantage of those same factors to avoid costs and, if possible, even profit from the situation. Eventually the crisis will be solved, for as a country with great political, economic and military power, the United States will not let itself go down. This article does not analyze the costs the United States could transfer to third countries but, from an internal perspective, examines who will pay for the mistakes made and which segments of the American society will emerge strengthened and which weakened or demolished. If the market is ferocious in normal times, one can imagine its voracity when the limits and possibilities are being violently restructured, allowing dramatic progresses and backward movements. The popular saying goes "it's good fishing in troubled waters"; yet in circumstances of crisis the winning fishermen are not usually the most honest, caring or concerned with the situation of the social whole, but rather the most skillful at making a profit at the expense of many others' disgrace. It is up to regulators and a conscious public to encourage those who are really contributing to the recovery and, at the same time, to limit the abuse and depredation, thus protecting the common citizen and, especially, the most vulnerable.

FAIR AND EFFECTIVE SOLUTIONS WHILE
WEATHERING THE STORM

The fact is that, faced with a crisis, the most daring actors take advantage of the fear and real risk of a generalized collapse to shape in their own interests the solutions that are designed to weather the storm. While the majority seeks refugee till the storm passes, the audacious make profits in the very course of the turbulence. They are not concerned with facing up to the direct consequences of what is going on. Rather they let public agencies, religious or development organizations, and common citizens assume them. Speculators have their energy free to profit from the juncture. In the countries of the South we have repeatedly seen that crises generate opportunities but that those opportunities are not democratically within everyone's reach.

Those with liquidity, contacts, and privileged information, usually profit outrageously, while the rest, cornered by the effects of the crisis, can barely focus on subsisting during the storm. When the turbulence passes, it is already too late to restore situations: the newly established dynamics are then harder to transform for everyone's benefit.

There is much to be safeguarded in a crisis, and this author is incapable of identifying all that needs to be done. I can only point out that the challenge lies not in surviving the storm but in taking advantage of, for the sake of the social body, or the opportunities forced by or born out of the present situation. In particular, given the focus of Opinion Sur on the base of the social pyramid, we can highlight some emergency measures to assist these sectors so that they can emerge strengthened rather than weakened from the crisis.

During the storm, and not after it, it is necessary to energize the productive mobilization of small producers; right away, with strength and determination. It is essential that the conditions for the functioning of the vast base of the US productive apparatus be strengthened by not only access to credit and capital, but also by providing information about good market opportunities and available modern business engineering. It is not a question of doing a little more of the same but by "the reshuffle and deal again" process that inherently comes with the crisis and gives way to something that is much better and sustainable.

The US counts with economic instruments to face an initiative of such significance and transcendence; yet the challenge's magnitude also demands reinforcing those instruments. Community Venture

Capital Funds already exist: they must be capitalized and replicated so as to take advantage of the experience accumulated in the last two decades. There are public and private programs aimed at small businesses; this is the time to increase their funding and exert the maximum tension on them. There is specialized small credit banking: it needs to develop even further and expand its coverage.

All this is possible and necessary. Yet there are some catalytic elements that can dramatically enrich the mobilization of the US huge productive base. Knowledge is their common denominator.

CATALYZING A BETTER WAY OUT
FROM THE PRESENT SITUATION

The US scientific and technological community is impressive. It may not be perfect and there is in fact a lot to be improved on, but the country's science and technology is a matchless instrument to effectively mobilize its productive base. In general, small producers have not been their main focus and, although no one could recommend that other areas of strategic importance be overlooked, the fact is that there is a great margin, until now poorly exploited, to mobilize the base of the social pyramid; that is, to facilitate the accelerated and sustainable development of a significant number of promising small ventures.

We emphasize the notion of "promising," which is associated with the concepts of excellence and opportunities, because it is not a question of reproducing mediocrity or non-sustainable ventures but rather to facilitate the best in the entrepreneurial and innovating spirit and allow it to germinate. Only that excellence, to acquire a significant magnitude, has to be raised not for a handful of initiatives but for the vast majority of small ventures. How can such a formidable and complex challenge be met? To begin with, it should not surprise us that it is with crises that the conditions to apply new solutions to old problems are created. Rather than giving a puzzled look on how recession and speculation advance, the scientific and technological community should declare itself in a state of emergency and support small entrepreneurs so that they may take advantage of the new economic spaces. Thus, instead of emerging from the present situation with an even more unequal society, the United States might find itself having a wider, more dynamic and creative productive base.

There are thousands, tens of thousands of entrepreneurs ready to face the challenge. There is not a lack of opportunities, but the conditions to take advantage of them should be available. One of those conditions is that development agencies and angel investor networks reinforce their social and economic knowledge of small entrepreneurs. If possible, they should bring in business engineering tools (such as franchise systems, export consortia, pools of service providers) capable of articulating disperse small production into medium-sized organizations that can access better opportunity thresholds. It will also help to create better links between angel investors and an increased number of venture capital community funds, to generate new good business developers to serve the base of the social pyramid, to multiply social innovation promotion mechanisms, to reorient business schools to better focus on small producers, to activate the meso-economic responsibility of leading corporations in productive chains so that they may explicitly include in their decision matrix the impact of their own actions upon suppliers, distributors and the communities where they do business (beyond the traditional public or corporate relations programs). It goes without saying that the role of the public sector becomes more important during crises, especially in the field of improving public spending allocation and eliminating regressive aspects of the tax system.

The list of possible actions and measures to best emerge from a crisis is endless. The guiding criterion, however, is to adhere adamantly to the principles the US people deem foundational to their identity and the future they wish to attain. The principles for normal times and those for moments of crisis do not differ. Crises do not require different principles but rather emergency measures aligned with those same principles. Freedom of thought and of the creation and management of initiatives, democratizing opportunities, preserving national unity, caring for the most vulnerable, assuming responsibility for our acts and for the consequences derived from them, are principles that do not go away with the crises; they are rather put to the test by it. Carrying this compass, Americans can explore new avenues to emerge strengthened and hopefully renewed from the crisis rather than to resort to costly bailouts that end up exacerbating serious phenomena of economic concentration.

CHAPTER VIII

Adjusting the Course

Among the factors that generated the present international crisis —some are evident such as the crisis-triggering debacle of the financial system— and some are less evident but equally important. Without the presence of these other factors this crisis is quite unlikely to have occurred, or its impacts would have been truncated. Which are those other factors? They are manifold, varied, and not restricted to just the economic world but also to governance and prevailing social attitudes.

Among the factors that generated the present international crisis some are evident —such as the crisis-triggering debacle of the financial system— and some are less evident but equally important. Without the presence of these other factors this crisis is quite unlikely to have occurred, or its impacts would have been truncated.

Which are those other factors? They are manifold, varied, and not restricted to just the economic world but also to governance and prevailing social attitudes. In the following lines some of the most important factors involved are analyzed and try to offer a wider vision of the nature of the crisis, its dynamics, and the measures that could help overcome it.

ECONOMIC FUNCTIONING BLOCKED BY INEQUALITY

A critical factor blocking economic functioning is the increased inequality that exists among countries and, within each country, among social sectors. This is a well-known and documented phenomenon.

Inequality is generated by a particular process of accumulation slanted towards the concentration of wealth. By this we imply that there are different types of accumulation processes: some of them generate an aggressive concentration of wealth, and others lead to a smaller or limited concentration.

It might seem that all accumulation processes are almost inherently prone to concentration unless different players intervene to offset such propensities and make decisions that are exogenous to the economic system.

The most significant decisions are those made at the government level to redistribute the flow of income, such as –among others– those related to the extent and distribution of the tax burden, the allocation of government spending, monetary and credit access policies, the ways in which national saving is channeled to different types of investment, and the adoption of social and environmental regulations.

Decisions made by companies, particularly by production chain leaders, in terms of wages, prices, technology, supply sources and destination of their products, also have a bearing on the prevailing type of accumulation. These strategic decisions produce primary effects impacting the company itself but also produce secondary effects on other economic players in the communities where they operate. Assessing these secondary effects and adjusting strategic decisions to maximize their positive impact are the pillars of what we call mesoeconomic responsibility of production chain leading firms.

The prevailing accumulation process has been, and still is, strongly concentrated, for multiple reasons of which include political and economic circumstance. Income concentration conditions the functioning of the economic system; it is a major factor impacting the economic dynamics leading to a crisis.

THE IMPACT OF CONCENTRATION ON THE CRISIS

I   To begin with, concentration leads to a segmentation of *effective demand*.

The affluent sectors, their bare necessities being fully met, are favoured by concentration and develop a conspicuous demand for often-superfluous goods that deepen social differences. This demand sends signals to the productive apparatus to produce these types of goods and services, generating a sub-optimal allocation of the national savings and creating, at the same time, corporate interests determined to sustain that consumption pattern and, indirectly, the concentration process underpinning it.

Low-income sectors that only partially manage to satisfy their basic needs coexist next to conspicuous consumption; thus they are only slightly expressed as effective demand. Middle-income groups, for their part, meet their basic needs and, when they have some balance left, generally reproduce –induced by advertising– a good portion of the superfluous consumption pattern.

II   At the same time, *those sectors that have benefited from the concentration process accumulate huge financial surpluses that need to be recycled.*

During normal times, people do not immobilize their surpluses; instead, they seek to place them in financial investments or the real economy in order to, given certain risk levels, obtain the greatest yield possible. Yet, the concentration process and its impacts on effective demand reduce the potential for opportunities in the real economy, and placements are shifted towards financial transactions that are ever more distant. For example, some financial transactions such as derivatives and mortgages are originally linked to the real economy, but the various transactional stages of these mechanisms dilute the responsibility and oversight due to a chain of entities that participate.

The financial system creates sophisticated products to absorb the surpluses in need of recycling, obtaining high returns in the process. But this modality establishes a dangerous vicious cycle that, if not altered, ends in collapse. To attract surplus resources, financial operators compete in terms of rates of return weighted according to each transactions risk. The greatest yields are obtained through bold financial engineering strategies and a certain concealment of implicit risks, as happened with sub-prime mortgages and other forms of consumer credit. With a non-expanding base of support, this process becomes inherently unsustainable.

III   How does the economic system react to the imbalances resulting from the concentration process?

One organic solution to ensure that production growth is maintained and does not become strangled is to reduce or reverse income concentration. This causes the consumer market to expand on the basis of genuine income while new opportunities are simultaneously generated in the real economy to productively absorb the existing financial resources.

Unfortunately, this is not the course being taken. Instead, and in the absence of an exogenous corrective intervention, the economic system seeks to extend its way of functioning without transforming its propensity towards concentration: rather than expanding the genuine income of middle and low-income sectors, it provides them with finance. Hence, after some credit cycles where consumers' debt grows at rates that exceed their income we almost inevitably end up in a pervasive situation of over-indebtedness.

The permanent recycling of surplus resources into financial transactions that are far removed from the real economy ends up generating explosive speculative bubbles that burst unexpectedly. In fact, rather than fighting or dismantling the concentration process and its effects, the economic dynamics ends up priming the pump, resulting in a destructive and painful explosion.

FUTILITY OF BAILOUTS THAT FAIL TO TRANSFORM THE WAY WE FUNCTION

The implication of this analysis about measures to overcome the crisis is very clear: it refers to the futility, or at least the insufficiency, of those measures incapable of transforming the concentrating pattern, which characterizes the way our economies operate. The truth is that by pumping in huge quantities of resources problems may be mitigated for some time regardless of the insufficiency of the adopted strategy. However problems will surface if those resources are not capable of altering the dynamics that lead to the crisis; when that happens the crisis will, sooner or later, reappear. Thus efforts end up being fruitless... perhaps not for all but, undoubtedly, for those who are forced to ultimately endure costly bailouts.

Which would be those corrective measures that might really contribute to overcoming the current crisis?

In response, those corrective measures that help produce the transition towards a non-concentrating accumulation are a good option. Among others,

I. Macro-policies to eliminate inequality and sustain growth in terms of fiscal policy, government spending, monetary stability, channeling saving towards real investment.

II. Meso-economic initiatives from leading firms in production networks intended to strengthen their value chains, ensuring a fair distribution of results among their members, and optimizing the secondary effects of their strategic decisions on other players.

III. Direct support to the bottom of the social and production pyramid by channeling knowledge of excellence, financing capital formation, assisting in the development of business management and sound structuring, and facilitating market access.

IMBALANCE BETWEEN GLOBAL ECONOMIC FORCES AND NATIONAL POLITICAL GOVERNANCE

The outburst of the international crisis encountered a world where economic forces have worldwide consequences, while political governance remains restricted to national boundaries. There was a gap between international economic development and international governance. This became absolutely evident at the onset of the global crisis: the initial reaction was uncoordinated and each country sought individual solutions. Soon they became aware it was not a single national economy but rather the central economies as a whole that were falling into the crisis with very probable repercussions on the rest of the developing world.

In the absence of a global government and in the face of the phenomenal uncontrolled proliferation of impacts, it became necessary to coordinate responses among countries, led by the United States and the European Union, with the less noticeable but absolutely critical involvement of China, India and the remaining Asian economic drivers.

The fact that there are global problems yet not global governance, adds a harsh restriction when it comes to facing the crisis and correcting the dynamics that generates it. It leads us to reflect upon institutional changes that should be tackled.

It will be necessary to attempt a transition towards a new international order that leaves extreme inequalities behind and is equipped with institutional governance that is properly articulated with national administrations. It would be something similar to what happened when, a long time ago in history, national governments were created and the city-states and other local jurisdictions were forced to adapt to the new circumstances.

Certainly, this transition is not easy, as it requires a great number of diverse interests to be reconciled. There are extremely complex subjects, such as those referred to identities and nationalities –preserving the differences and diversities with the greatest of respects–, and the allocation of functions among local, national and global levels. The issue is to address global problems without trimming jurisdictions so that national or local problems can be tackled effectively; a complex and controversial topic due to the close interaction among levels that blurs the borders of what is global, national and local. In spite of all these complexities it will be nevertheless necessary to explore ways to move forward in that transition.

A BAFFLED SOCIETY

Contemporary acceleration and rapid transformations affect all social layers (certainly young and indigent people all the more), generating an ever more disconcerted society. An astonished look at their problems and challenges prevails, the opposite side of the same coin beings a slow response capacity to find solutions, which leads to greater anxiety, confusion and alienation taking the form of addictions (alcohol, drugs, gaming, consumerism), expressions of nihilism, intolerance, aggressiveness, social and domestic violence.

A disconcerted society contributes to sustaining the dynamics leading to the crisis; it entails a weakness to understand, resist and adjust behaviours. It facilitates will-power manipulation and the development of a culture of fear that, when a crisis bursts out, easily turns into panic that enormously magnifies the impact of the crisis.

On the face of this situation, what counts is to put forth a permanent effort to throw light, help understand complex dynamics, identify better choices, strengthen self-confidence and resilience, motivate to face and overcome difficulties. Actions oriented towards raising individual and group awareness, reinforcing values adapted to the present historic phase of humanity.

No magical potion will solve the confusion, and no enlightened whomsoever will either. Instead, daily efforts made by public, private and civil society players to articulate reflection, strategic thinking and transforming action on all fronts of our social and political life will help.

Part Two

GETTING OUT OF THE CRISIS TOWARDS A SUSTAINABLE DEVELOPMENT

CHAPTER IX

Did we deserve the crisis?

The crisis explodes and we rush to take shelter from the rainstorm. While we do, the process seeks to find its course, as a crisis does not stop, but transforms the social and economic dynamics. So big is the fear and confusion that only the daring or those who are best positioned, understand that this is the time to apply energy to channel the situation in one direction or another. What happened and why did it happen? Could the crisis have been avoided? Did blindness precipitate it? What comes next? How do we react? We must ask ourselves whether we want to change; immediately after we will find out whether we will be capable of changing.

The crisis explodes and we rush to take shelter from the rainstorm. While we do this, the process seeks to find its course, as a crisis does not stop, but transforms the social and economic dynamics. In this flow of events, powerful interests struggle so that the outcome may turn as much in their favour as possible. So big is the fear and confusion that only the daring or those who are best positioned, understand that this is the time to apply energy to channel the situation in one direction or another.

WHAT HAPPENED AND WHY IT HAPPENED

The diagnosis of why the crisis burst out begins by pointing out that the financial system exhibited a lousy behaviour, and made it possible for sectors without repayment capacity to become indebted. What is not sufficiently elucidated is the reason for such behaviour and the resulting over-indebtedness.

In my opinion, one of the key factors that precipitated the crisis was the mismatch that had occurred between the rate of growth in production supply and the rate of growth of those who absorb that production (effective demand). This was the result of a concentration-oriented growth that led to increasing inequity in almost all world economies. It is worth mentioning that such inequity occurred not only in emerging economies (translated into greater poverty and indigence) but also in central economies having much higher standards of living, and it was there where the present crisis started.

As it turned out, the "organic" growth of the economic system was hurt (a relatively balanced growth of its key variables). Apart from praiseworthy exceptions, analysts in the Northern Hemisphere who operate from the perspective of abundance and growth reproduction as well as those in the south who operate from the perspective of shortage and development promotion had underestimated the critical role that inequity plays by affecting the foundations of organic economic growth.

Inequity implies several things. On the one hand, that there exists a certain lag or backwardness in the incomes of middle and low-income sectors (workers, small producers, retirees, the unemployed, marginalized population in large cities, towns and rural areas) in relation to the growth in production and the economy in aggregate terms. This lag translates, in the Southern countries, in extended poverty, while in the Northern countries the relative lag may occur even with an improvement in absolute terms in the general standard of living. There is a gap, a disconnection between the total goods and services that a vibrant productive apparatus is capable of producing and what the demand is capable of absorbing. We are talking about gaps in aggregate terms because sector or territorial gaps are in fact being constantly produced in the economy, but they manage to be absorbed –"resolved"– by trade, migrations, the overall economic dynamics through innovations and permanent restructuring.

Those gaps generate tensions and if the latter acquire a systemic dimension, they can no longer be solved by the sole economic dynamics and require the intervention of regulators and political helmsmen. If these do not react making timely decisions that go beyond the purely functional ones, the functioning of the economic machinery gets blocked and crises break out.

Inequity also involves a growing concentration of savings, that portion of income that is not spent and may be used to finance investment, which is one of the pillars of economic growth. Depending on how savings are channeled, "allocated", one or another type of investment will result: a more productive investment, or a more financial and speculative one; an investment that is concentrated on large economic players, or a deconcentrated investment that contributes to capital formation among small and medium-sized producers; an investment that threatens the environment, or an investment that safeguards and protects it.

The concentration of savings takes place at the same time that investment opportunities in the real economy diminish as a result of the reduction of the demand with respect to production. This gap gets worse due to the superfluous nature of the consumption of those who concentrate incomes, which is spread through aggressive advertising to the rest of society.

Thus, the concentration of savings and the reduction in investment opportunities in the real economy combine to deviate funds towards financial products that are ever more speculative and, hence, entail higher returns and risks, risks that are sought to be concealed under different types of derivatives. The logic of recycling concentrated savings by luring them with juicy yields and hiding the inherent risk to this type of financial schemes led to a blurring of the ethical limits, giving way to bold or even criminal adventures.

THE CRISIS IS AVOIDABLE

It is clear that it is possible to prevent the economic functioning from ending in a crisis. This goes beyond regulating the financial markets appropriately, which is certainly necessary to do. When economic forces that hit the borders of the economic system's sustainability unleash, strengthening the defenses is not enough; it also becomes necessary to deactivate those forces that are social and not natural. It is required to work on an organic growth that avoids the traumatic effects of the inequity produced by concentrating processes; among other factors, try to make the consumers' genuine income grow hand by hand with the supply of goods and services. This will contribute to a better growth of the economy that, however, will never be exempt from occasional imbalances and turbulences that are inherent to complex systems where millions of players interact. Those tensions can be "absorbed" within the regular functioning of the economic system; that is, without trespassing the functional limits of sustainability and avoiding falling into recurrent crises.

Oftentimes, maybe even most of the times, markets do not manage to ensure sustained organic growth on their own as diverse factors tend to trigger beyond the proportions required for a relatively balanced growth to occur. It is in those moments when regulating the systemic functioning becomes a must in order to guarantee its efficacy and gear it towards benefiting society as a whole.

Countless policies, mechanisms, and instruments may be used to such end. This battery of measures includes eliminating regressive tax systems and reducing tax evasion; implementing a fairer, more efficient allocation of government spending, a monetary policy that secures price stability, regulates financial intermediation and promotes credit access; channeling national saving so that it may further enable capital formation at the bottom of the productive apparatus; implementing direct actions to support small producers in relation to knowledge, contacts, market access and modern business engineering; promoting equitable linkages between production chain leading firms and suppliers, distributors and clients, so as to exert the leading firms full meso-economic responsibility.

THE BLINDNESS THAT PRECIPITATES THE CRISIS

Nonetheless, for a long time it was not wanted, possible or simply ignored, to address the challenges that establishing an organic growth entails. In particular, income distribution worsened instead of improving and, to tackle the widening gaps, the solution sought consisted in extending credit instead of generating more genuine income among middle and low-income sectors (the base of the social pyramid). The approach made it possible for inequity to continue to grow, with the resulting concentration of income, saving and investment. Myopia became an accomplice to avarice and mean-spiritedness. Some warned about the tensions that kept building up under the surface; yet, since "growth" was vigorous and appeared to be sustained, few were willing to believe that such course and way of functioning would end up being unsustainable.

Meanwhile, dissatisfaction was being dodged, postponed, by causing the middle-income, and to a lesser extent, the low-income sectors to become indebted. At that time over-indebtedness raised no concern at all. Why should it worry anyone if, thanks to it, the economic machinery was going through a period of great bonanza?

Besides, there was politics, to manage occasional outbursts, and the large media, to homogenize thought and stifle dissent.

The dreadful financial bubbles were thus gradually formed, ever more aloof from the man in the street's economy. The financial system grew self-centered; financial "products" mobilized huge amounts of money that could be transferred massively and in real time by just being equipped with communication facilities; the returns offered outperformed any other investment choice in the real economy. The conditions were converging for a large systemic crisis to unfold.

THE BLAST AND WHAT IS TO COME

And, alas! One fine day, the shockwave of that frenzied speculative allocation of saving began to burst the huge financial bubbles, unveiling, in the first place, the existence of mortgage and credit card over-indebtedness and, as a result of that, impacting in domino-effect fashion on the rest of the markets. Bubbles deflated as quickly as our children or grandchildren's balloons do.

That over-indebtedness would have produced less harm or maybe a positive impact if it had been directed to more meaningful consumption, away from the superficiality of needs that are not basic which are encouraged and supported by highly effective commercial advertising. Another economic dynamic could have developed –way distanced from financial speculation and with a much more rational allocation of available resources– had we changed the profile of our consumption orienting it instead to one of clean energy, healthy food, preventive medicine, goods that do not encourage further existential alienation and slippery into addictions; a consumption that carries values and not ostentation that exacerbates social differentiation. In other words, the outcome would have been different had consumerism been replaced by responsible consumption

Inequity not only applies to income, it also manifests itself in the existence of knowledge, information, contacts, market and capital access gaps, which jeopardizes personal development and capital formation in small and micro producer sectors that constitute vast majorities in almost all our countries. This does not necessarily have to be this way, as it was assumed in the past when it was taken for granted that economies of scale were an insurmountable constraint. Today, however, we have access to modern business engineering that is capable of structuring scattered small production into medium-sized organizations capable of accessing higher opportunity thresholds. This is the case of franchising, export consortia, centralized service providers, modern production networks led by well-organized enterprises that propel the growth of the entire value chain. However, little of that reaches the bottom of the pyramid, which instead of excellence receives what is left over, or the scrap.

THE WAY WE REACT AND ITS PROBABLE CONSEQUENCES

In the face of a crisis, very different measures are available to mitigate its effects and try to cause the river to return to its course, which would be a crass mistake to make: the river should not return to "that" course, because we would be once again reconstructing the scenario and the dynamics that led to the crisis. Let us not be confused, the king was naked, even if we did not dare to acknowledge that.

The key measures being discussed are intended to underpin the financial system as it, in point of fact, is a part of the nervous system of any economy. Huge amounts of money are devoted to "bail out" banks, insurance companies, and mortgage agencies. So many are the billions that the ordinary citizen cannot even retain the figures, let alone figure out what such phenomenal reorientation of resources implies in terms of opportunity costs.

In addition to that, consumption stimulus plans are being presented, as the productive apparatus sees with justified terror that the enormous contraction in demand threatens its subsistence. The market dries up, and so does the destination of its production, although, it must be made clear, not all will be affected in the same way. Those who produce steel, cement, aluminum, oil, equipment, machinery, etc, will depend on new public work programs, which will become the key productive and social investment drivers; those who produce essential goods (food, drugs, communications, etc.), which are indispensable even during a crisis, will have better prospects than those who are devoted to the production of superfluous mass consumer goods (during a crisis, the room for irresponsible consumption is reduced, as urgencies relocate family priorities); with one exception: the production of superfluous goods intended for high-income sectors will survive, because the wealthiest 10% of the planet's population will maintain their standard of living with very few cutbacks.

But, how can consumption be encouraged among those who see their income drop and unemployment grow? The first reaction is to allocate public funds to the withdrawal of "toxic assets" and the establishment of new finance lines, loosening conditions to access those credits. It is not a question of generating genuine income; that will be done "once the storm has been weathered". At this point in time the main challenge is deemed to consist in "pump-priming"; bringing the machinery back into operation; causing supply –that supply generated by the existing productive apparatus– to meet a demand that is capable of absorbing its production so that it may then be able to re-generate employment, reducing rampant unemployment, calming the waters, gaining back the "confidence" of all of us in the economic system.

Yet, wouldn't we then be fixing that particular machinery, that functional logic, that systemic rationality that led us to the crisis? Wouldn't we be producing another round of over-indebtedness, of consumerism, of income, saving and power concentration, of a frenzied pursuit of benefits, of institutions threatened by privileges, arbitrariness, aggravated criminal systems?

DID WE DESERVE THE CRISIS?

The answer is a categorical "yes". But we are not talking about deserving the crisis as a punishment but, instead, as a consequence of the way we had become organized as society, the way we functioned. By favouring certain aspects and ignoring others, we established a certain economic order; we set up priorities and oblivions.

It is difficult to steer an economy that rewards mean-spiritedness and avarice as the basis for accumulation. Accumulation is indispensable for economic functioning, but it needs not be aggressively concentration-oriented; there may be accumulation distributed among all layers of the social and economic structure: large, medium and small-sized enterprises. If capital formation grew excessively in large units, we would no doubt be creating an inevitable concentration process, as the very economic dynamics would be taking –as it actually takes– that course.

The challenge lies in thinking of new ways of structuring ourselves and of functioning because that is what we are talking about when we refer to coming out of a crisis stronger. If we are paying such a price for mistakes we have made, let us look for opening new opportunities. We need to establish a different set of prizes and punishment; one that promotes those who add value to the social effort and not those who speculate and profit from the rest; to encourage those who organize production differently, acknowledge what each one contributes to the social functioning: the ordaining and regulating State, responsible entrepreneurs, workers and civil society, including educators, scientists, technological innovators; those that shape values such as social, religious and political leaders, the media, advertising agencies and, in each home, parents or "that significant other". An optimistic, though not naïve vision of the human condition would indicate that we will know how to stand tall above our own mistakes, reflect, and grow in terms of experience, take care of one another, exercise our free will acknowledging limits. These are potentialities that speak of doing as well as being, but they do not guarantee per se any given course. We must individually ask ourselves whether we really want to change; immediately after we will find out whether we will be capable of changing.

This year we are celebrating astronomy, and we marvel at the wonders of the universe, its complexity and countless enigmas. Confronted with that enormity, it is awesome that "earthly" matters may also be so highly complex and that, within our own selves and our societies, enigmas are nested just as impenetrable as those remote galaxies and the big bang. We bear a changing and tempestuous mix of needs, interests, values, and emotions. With it, and with our capacity to think and act we can be able to give way to something better for the future that starts today. We deserved the crisis, but what matters now is whether we will know how to transform it into an opportunity.

CHAPTER X

Transforming in the spur of the moment

Every crisis entails an opportunity, granted; but an opportunity is a possibility, not a certainty and, hence, if we do not seize it, we lose it. Although painful, the most valuable opportunity that a crisis brings along is precisely the possibility of transforming for the better what was in existence. It is in the course of the emergency, when worry and perplexity shake us that the restructuring options start being defined. Later, when the lava cools down, the new relations among players, the new ways of functioning, the new paths consolidate and it becomes harder to shape the transformation. A transformation implies carrying out a series of tasks; it is a complex and fascinating effort of interpreting reality, projecting the future, causing interests to converge, mobilizing wills and organizing action.

Every crisis entails an opportunity, granted; but an opportunity is a possibility, not a certainty and, hence, if we do not seize it, we lose it. The opportunity does not come out to meet us if we become paralyzed and seek cover in the basement until the storm subsides. On the contrary, it will be necessary to come out to meet it while the crisis is in progress, and work in order to take advantage of it.

We pointed out in previous chapters that even though the malfunctioning of the financial system triggered the present crisis, other critical factors converged to generate it. In most of the cases, it is necessary to adjust what we do, and how we do it, rather than merely reconstructing what was in existence. A crisis involves a drastic change of circumstances, some of them evident such as costs and pervasive destruction, while others, originated with the adjustment of profound plates of reality, are more difficult to read. The change of circumstances calls for new paths and the initiation of a transformation-building process. It is in this juncture of pain and confusion that it is necessary to transform our course and way of functioning.

THE TASK OF BUILDING A TRANSFORMATION

Among other factors, social, productive, technological, international trade development constantly foster transformations; yet social decisions are the ones that set the course and mold of our way of functioning through a change in attitudes, policies and regulations. When a crisis bursts, the first reactions tend to avoid or mitigate impacts. Fear and anguish in the face of uncertainty obscure the fact that our way of reacting before the crisis lays the foundations for what will come after the trauma.

The strength of the economic tsunami disrupts processes and relations in such a way that opens spaces to develop new courses that were previously unthinkable. It is in the course of the emergency when worries and perplexity shake us that the restructuring options start being defined. Later, when the lava cools down, the new relations among players, the new ways of functioning, the new paths consolidate and it becomes harder to shape the transformation. *Although painful, the most valuable opportunity that a crisis brings along is precisely the possibility of transforming for the better what was in existence.*

HOW TO WORK IN THE MIDDLE OF A CRISIS IN ORDER TO BUILD A TRANSFORMATION THAT MAY ENABLE US TO SEIZE OPPORTUNITIES?

Various are the work fronts that need to be addressed in the spur of the moment, among others, the task of interpreting reality, projecting the future, making interests converge, mobilizing wills, and organizing action. This is not related to a lineal sequence but to stages that need to be tackled almost simultaneously in order to feed and improve each work front with the information and results that crop up from the rest.

(A)   The task of interpreting reality

Although at times not well valued, this is a fundamental space. There always exist various possible interpretations of a same and single reality depending on the analytical framework used to assess it. Some will highlight certain aspects and will acknowledge certain logics of societal functioning while others will choose different interpretative variables and produce alternative explanations of the socio economic dynamic. Although there may be common denominators, it is worthwhile to recognize and accept that there is a diversity of diagnostic outlooks on one same process. Some ignore that diversity of interpretations and believe they are the owners of the only right view. This occurs in authoritarian or fundamentalist regimes but also in democracies, when powerful interests with major media support back certain viewpoints. In these cases, the quality of the line of argument, the analytical rigor and the capacity to explain facts of each interpretation carry no weight: what counts is how strong the backing for each interpretation is. When support sources are strongly concentrated, there is a greater risk of slipping towards homogeneous thinking, which impoverishes and narrows the capacity to understand what is going on, as well as to sustain more effective proposals for action. In this "ranking of credibility" the valuable contribution of analysts who only rely on their acute insight into processes is lost. Between the teams who are backed by major media and those having independent views there exist huge disparities in terms of resources and the capacity to make them heard.

In any case, the process of building an effective transformation is based in the first place on an appropriate appreciation of what is going on in the light of the chosen course. This entails selecting adequate interpretative variables, assessing the correlation of forces, recognizing parameters, foreseeing their possible changes in the mid term, and adequately processing the available information.

For instance, some of us consider that inequality and poverty are structural imbalances of the economic system and one of the main causes that generated the current crisis. Others, instead, do not deny the existence of those dramatic imbalances yet do not take them as logical results of the prevailing course and way of functioning and even less as one of the causes that led to the crisis. Each interpretation of the same phenomenon will lead to very different ways of projecting the future, making interests converge, mobilizing wills and organizing action.

(B) The task of projecting the future

Looking at the future is in some sense shaping it so that we can have a guide in the twilight of new situations. Depending on how we envision it, we will influence our courses of action. It is as though the future would influence the present.

We can project the future following the historic trend, or introducing inflection points based on changes of circumstances and society's willingness to build a transformation. Within this range determinism and voluntarism are equally dangerous extremes.

In determinism destiny is prefigured, which has the twofold implication of preserving the status quo and discouraging the will to change. Certainly, there exist contextual parameters that must be inevitably taken into consideration, as the same impose restrictions that condition the course; ignoring or failing to assess them properly may cause our best intention to fail. But it is also certain that, even within those parameters (which, by the way, change with time) we have room to exercise our free will.

In voluntarism we overestimate our capacity to change reality failing to properly assess the contextual parameters as well as the correlation of forces within which we must act. Errors of judgment compromise the intended transformation and negatively affect the social forces promoting it.

Building a transformation involves generating a chain of inflection points in our path as a society, in order to adjust our march towards a view of the future (guiding utopia) that hints at another possible, desirable reality. This long-term guide makes it possible to plan an attainable mid-term considering an adjustment in the systemic direction and a continuous effort to make our way of functioning more efficient.

A better course and effective functioning are the fundamental pillars of any transformation. And as we have just pointed out they are based on how we interpret reality and project the future. However, in order to materialize the process of building a transformation, it is also indispensable to cause interests to converge, mobilize wills and organize action.

(C) The task of causing interests to converge

A society always has multiple interests that at times complement and at other times antagonize one with each other. To the extent that more and more interests converge on a same path, larger will be the social energy channeled towards transformation instead of sterilized in struggles among antagonists that only seek to make their own interests prevail.

Some consider the dynamics between disparate interests as a zero-sum process. In other words, what one gains is, inevitably, what the other one loses; hence, the only way to assert my interests is by crushing those of the rest in order to broaden my own realization space. This usually happens in severely imperfect, ill-regulated markets, most particularly, in times of crises or strong economic recession. In these situations –indeed, today we are going through one of the worst global crises of our times– the strongest, best-informed individuals seek to dump on others their own share of costs and responsibilities.

This, however, must not inevitably be this way. With political leadership and an intensive use of regulatory instances it is possible to find formulas to align interests, cause them to converge into solutions, ensuring that costs are minimized and that the possible results of a transformation are fairly shared. This is a difficult task, because we are not dealing with generous players; instead, we are faced with tough, though ultimately always pragmatic, interests.

If the alignment of interests is approached as in a static context, the room for solutions becomes reduced. But if agreements on interests were to be situated in a dynamic context, spaces to converge would broaden considerably. Even then, furthering the convergence of interests is a tough task, one in which it is necessary to combine firmness with creativity and cleverness. The convergence of interests cannot be left to spontaneity as it seldom happens; without a view of the whole and a leadership that works to generate convergence, each particular interest will tend to follow a self-centered course. The task of making interests converge requires a good understanding of the interests at stake, recognizing existing limits, choosing appropriate ways of approximation, equipping oneself with tools of persuasion, and producing win-win solutions where all parties come to share results.

Yet, even with an accurate interpretation of reality, with a consistent set of mid-term projections, with an effective interest alignment and convergence effort, a transformation cannot be actually materialized if two critical tasks are not tackled: the task of mobilizing wills and the task of organizing action.

(D)   The task of mobilizing wills

Mobilizing wills involves knowing how to inspire and guide the different players in a society. It implies understanding their motivations, knowing their longings and fears; mastering a diversity of languages, idiosyncrasies and imaginaries, exercising leadership by integrating efforts and generating synergies, which does not mean to pile up initiatives but to articulate them in a constructive way.

Wills may be mobilized on the basis of deception, although the resulting dynamics is usually short-lived. With time, inconsistencies and frustrations undermine the will to accompany a process that becomes distorted and does not satisfy deeply felt needs.

Charismatic leaders generate enthusiasm, which makes the mobilization effort easier. Yet, effective political scaffolding and a good mid-term project expressing the alignment of interests are required in order to sustain the mobilization. The task of mobilizing wills requires permanence and credibility; discontinuous efforts undermine its efficacy generating voids that are hard to recover. To arouse enthusiasm and full participation it will be necessary to soak into those values and longings that are most deeply felt by communities.

(F) **The task of organizing action**

The task of organizing action is very diverse and involves all social players, the public sector, businesses and entrepreneurs, civil society organizations, the media, trade associations and unions, to mention but a few. It requires planning but also operational flexibility so that we do not prevent quick responses to the permanent and unexpected changes of circumstances. This involves having to live with a constant tension between seeing to it that what was agreed upon is fulfilled and consenting to changes being made as we go along if reality so requires. If this tension is properly resolved, effectiveness will be gained. The downside here, however, is the risk of facilitating arbitrary action and funds diversion. It is not easy to strike a fair balance as the key lies in exercising good judgment, only that those who must exercise it are, at the same time, imperfect individuals having interests, needs and emotions. Thus there exists an inevitable twofold demand: ensuring ever-greater policy rationality and efficiency, coupled with the need to choose the most rigorous, honest leaders.

Making things happen is no easy task; it has to do with doing what is deemed necessary to generate and sustain a transformation but, in addition and as it was mentioned above, doing it with efficacy, that is, accomplishing what has been proposed with the lowest possible organizational and financial costs or, reversing the perspective, given a certain level of organizational and financial input, attaining the greatest possible impact.

The task of organizing, and then supervising, action faces us with tough issues such as corruption, diversion of funds and energies towards a patronage system, and organizational negligence. A poor leadership and management supervision may sterilize any transformation-building effort.

The task of organizing action must assign a preponderant role to innovation, to refurbishing institutions in synch with the present times, to creating instruments that are ever more effective and most fit for the reality that is intended to be transformed. Each historical phase requires a new generation of instruments. For instance, if reduction of inequity and poverty is a central goal (not just a marginal program) then we will have to give way to new strategies, policies and instruments, including (I) realigning the macro-economic policy (tax, public spending, monetary) in favour of the base of the social pyramid, (II) mobilizing productive chains leading businesses toward inclusive courses of action so that they fully exercise their meso-economic responsibility, (III) developing a battery of actions in direct support of the bottom of the social and economic pyramid, placing emphasis on capital formation and the streamlining of the way in which small and medium-sized firms are run. To make the latter feasible, traditional instruments must be supplemented with other new-fledged ones that are tailored to local circumstances, such as inclusive business developers, socially and environmentally responsible angel investor networks and local funds to support productive investments. There is not lack of talent or determination to work in our Southern countries, but support systems are poor in terms of ensuring that our majorities emerge and realize their full potential.

It is worthwhile to close this chapter reasserting that transformations are not something magical. Although there is room for charisma, ideals, will power, commitment, determination, and the longing of each one, all factors that have a strong bearing, a transformation implies carrying out a series of tasks. It is a fascinating work of interpreting reality, projecting the future, causing interests to converge, mobilizing wills and organizing action. This is the reason why we say that a transformation is not dreamed of or awaited; it is built.

CHAPTER XI

Decision-making to come out of the crisis

Who take part in the decision making process to come out of the crisis; what are the prevailing ideas on approaches and measures; which ones will be finally adopted?

PARTICIPANTS IN THE DECISION-MAKING PROCESS

Ultimately, the representatives of national governments are the ones who make the key decisions to come out of the crisis, depending on the political weight that each country carries within the international commonwealth. Countries carrying the greatest weight are grouped in the so-called *G-20* (now 22); they account for 80% of both the world's GDP and world trade, and two-thirds of the global population. There exist pressures associated with having countless players with different degrees of influence that converge on leaders.

It is clear that the policies that led to the crisis benefited the financial sector of central countries and emerging economies: they accumulated huge economic power and great political influence. For instance, up until 1982 the benefits of the financial sector in the US were similar to those of the other industrial sectors; then the benefits of the financial sector expanded until becoming, in 2007, 85% higher than the rest of the industry. During that period of expansion of their benefits the financial sector, with the support of mainstream think tanks and the media, resisted policy changes aimed at controlling them. Crowning that influence, Wall Street investment bankers were conducting national economic policy from the Department of the Treasury and the Federal Reserve in Washington, DC.

Although affected by the crisis they helped generate, big financial groups still preserve a high level of influence as, should they collapse, they would drag down many other companies and families in their fall. Other important economic sectors that have been less damaged by the crisis, such as communications, health, food, or those that play a strategic role, such as armaments and energy industries, oil and gas in particular, also maintain great capacity to exert influence on the shaping of new global policies. Although there are certain organizations that struggle for the interest of the average citizen, ordinary taxpayers do not have any other formal representative than their government. Should governments turn away from them, the great majorities (hundreds of millions of people) would not have anyone to defend their interests and needs at the negotiating table. The new architecture of the international economic system and the new policies that will guide its way of functioning will be very much influenced by those who end up seated at the drawing board.

The crisis generated a certain shift in terms of decision-making from the economic to the political ground, which makes room for considering other approaches and measures. Yet, if such room is not duly taken advantage of, we will end up reproducing, with only cosmetic changes, the same processes that resulted in this huge global crisis.

PREVAILING IDEAS ABOUT APPROACHES AND MEASURES

Even though there are new ideas and perspectives, mainstream think tanks continue to carry greater weight due to their position in the most important communication nodes; hence, and not necessarily due to the merit of their analyses and argumentations, they are paid more heed than other engines of strategic thinking.

One of the driving ideas that mainstream think tanks proclaim is the immediate need to bail out the existing financial system. They act on the urgency that the situation indeed imposes, and elude discussing a thorough transformation of the structure and way of functioning of financial intermediation. The backbone of the proposals consists in "recovering" the solvency and credibility of financial institutions, ridding them of the so-called toxic assets; "re-establishing" credit without affecting the corporate structure, nor ensuring that two-thirds of the world population have full credit access, nor obliterating the criminal nonsense of tax havens, nor securing an effective monitoring of all financial products, hedge funds included.

Another key idea is that of expanding global demand by pumping government funds into the market. This would be attained by (I) offering public sector financed credit lines, in order to substitute the declining propensity to lend of institutions that have been so severely hit by the crisis, and (II) generating activities via ambitious plans in social and productive infrastructure. Once again, the devil is in the details and its tail may only be noticed when these measures are disaggregated and studied in detail.

Ideas striving to be considered

One of the main notions that call to be considered in the present agenda is the critical role inequity played –socially and among countries– in generating the crisis. Inequity was the result of a specific growth pattern that derived in concentrated (and concentrating) accumulation of wealth, income, savings and investment. There are other ways to grow that lead to a much more balanced and de-concentrated accumulation, promoting a better distribution of wealth, income, savings and investment, and with significant effects on what is produced, who produces it, how it is produced, when it is produced, as well as what, who, how and where it is consumed. The coming out of the crisis is a golden opportunity to change the production and consumption pattern, so that efficient production that does not harm the environment may be encouraged, that consumerism may be replaced by responsible consumption, and that scientific and technological development may be accordingly oriented. As public funding and regulations are so preponderant in this phase, the capacity to adjust the systemic course has increased considerably.

There also exist serious doubts about the proposed financial bailout, in the sense that it might constitute a subtle way of ensuring the survival of the financial class that profited limitlessly and with few regulations until the crisis burst. To prevent this from happening, a bailout based on other grounds is propounded, whereby a restructuring of the financial system may be ensured. This restructuring of the financial system would induce another course subject to a more effective regulatory framework but without affecting, however, the dynamics and innovation required to keep up with constantly changing circumstances. This might lead to reorganization of the huge financial entities that had concentrated large market shares and attained enormous economic and political power. The "cleansing" of toxic assets and the establishment of new regulatory standards provide each country's financial authority with powerful instruments to create a new effective and vigorous financial system.

A MORE APPROPRIATE DECISION-MAKING STRUCTURE

The international crisis puts to the test the decision-making structure existing in the world. There are large global decisions that need to be considered, and there are also other multiple decisions at the national and local levels. The whole decision-making system is under strain, even if the same is not clearly structured. Structures originated in past international junctures are being used to give way to new structures that may best adjust to the enormous changes that occurred in recent decades. As always, it is necessary to change as we go along, with prudence, without arbitrariness, and weighing all legitimate interests at stake. Leaps in the dark do not help; instead, they cause a regression in the improvement processes.

The current systemic functioning is based on what today exists but adjusting the course and achieving a better way of functioning will be the result of projecting and organizing new structures, whose viability will depend upon how well the present correlation of international forces may install its vision, needs, values and interests.

CHAPTER XII

G-20 Proposals to Address the Crisis: Restoration or Transformation?

The proposals of the Group of 20 included in the London Summit statement reflect the tugging and forced consensuses negotiated within that boiling kettle. The central countries focused on their own needs, side-glancing the rest of the world. But just as pompous, politically correct declarations that end up being too difficult to materialize are of no use, and it would also be of no use to criticize without recognizing that any headway at all is being made. This article analyzes the proposed course of action and intends to recognize the direction that is beginning to take shape.

The proposals of the Group of 20 included in the London Summit statement reflect the tugging and forced consensuses negotiated within that boiling kettle. The central countries focused on their own needs, side-glancing the rest of the world. But just as pompous, politically correct declarations that end up being too difficult to materialize are of no use, it would also be of no use to criticize without recognizing that any headway at all is being made. The London Summit statement points out that a global crisis requires a global solution, which is partially true. The crisis being global requires an effective coordination of national efforts, although each country's circumstances are so unique that the way and virulence with which the crisis manifests imposes treatments with some common denominators, and many more measures customized to the requirements of each specific reality.

In turn, the responsibilities for having generated the crisis are not homogeneous; there were countries and sectors that, having benefited to a greater extent than the rest in the pre-crisis period, were directly responsible not only for creating the conditions that led to the crisis but also for triggering it. Those countries and sectors should assume a larger share of the damage they caused and the cost of coming out of the crisis they helped to generate. It is a principle of justice that it be so, although in general everyone, and especially the most powerful players, seeks to pass the responsibility and costs on other shoulders. They have access to subtle economic mechanisms that allow reaching results nobody would dare to claim openly.

These lines analyze the proposed course of action in an attempt to recognize the implicit direction that is beginning to take shape:

It is true that to be constant, growth has to be shared. This is what the London statement proclaims when it states that "our global plan for recovery must have at its heart the needs and jobs of hard-working families, not just in developed countries, but also in emerging markets and the poorest countries of the world; and must reflect the interests, not just of today's population, but of future generations too" (semicolons inserted by us).

What does this expression imply, that we will all grow at the same rate and thus reproduce the current inequity? Or are we open to promoting the higher growth of the poorest countries and the small and medium sized emerging economies in order to start closing the huge income and opportunity gap that exists at the global level?

Almost at the end, the statement addresses this question by stating, "We are determined not only to restore growth, but also to lay the foundations for a fair and sustainable world economy." Then, it reaffirms the commitment to meeting the so far ill-accomplished Millennium Development Goals, and lists the actions to be channeled through the UN, the IMF, the World Bank, regional banks, the ILO, and the UN Climate Change Conference, to be held at the end of this year. This proposal resembles the conventional approach used to tackle inequity and poverty, which more or less would consist in: Let us, who have clout and voice, talk about our own growth problems, about the global economic dynamics, and then consequently define strategies, policies and measures and, this being solved or somewhat made clear, devote one special chapter that is separated, segregated from the core measures, to inequity and poverty. It is as though the economy and the main interests of those who lead the process on an international level and within the countries flowed, while somewhere else along the margins, goes the economy and interests of the large majorities of contemporary world. This is not the way in which shared growth is accomplished. Inequity, poverty, and a fair and sustainable economic system need to be addressed from and through the main variables and not through a specific action that merely complements the core strategies: These actions and variables include world trade (with the essential safeguards for the development of new competitive advantages in small and mid-sized emerging economies), a balanced capital flow, the decentralized location of productive activities, adequate labour migration, and strong cooperation and funding (including subsidies) by central countries in order to help the Southern Hemisphere countries establish a vigorous scientific and technological development. What is required is not a "special program" but, rather, an adjustment of the systemic course and of our way of functioning that may lead to a fairer, more sustainable international and national order.

The London Summit statement also points out that "the only sure foundation for sustainable globalization and rising prosperity for all is an open world economy based on market principles, effective regulation, and strong global institutions". The crisis has made it clear that the market is a formidable resource-allocating agent as long as the social and economic dynamics do not slide towards a process of wealth, income, savings, and investment concentration, or towards environmental destruction. A good market is capable of solving many things, but not those that over conditioned it. In order to influence the context and ensure a systemic course beneficial for our society as a whole, political decisions such as the ones the G 20 was forced to tackle are needed.

The definition of the systemic course goes beyond the exercise of effective regulation and the establishment of strong global institutions, these two factors being of utmost importance. The issue is that if we manage to set a good systemic course, then it does become imperative to have effective regulation and strong global institutions to ensure that such a course is respected and the systemic way of functioning is effective, agile, and strengthened by innovations based on an adequate scientific and technological development. If, instead, the systemic course ends up being one that reproduced inequity, environmental deterioration, and unfair and non-sustainable development, then what would be the use of having regulations or strong institutions, unless we used them to guard that ill-fated course that led us into the crisis in the first place?

In the London Summit statement, the G-20 members pledge to "do whatever is necessary to restore confidence, growth, and jobs; repair the financial system to restore lending; strengthen financial regulation to rebuild trust..." (Italics added by us). Note that the verbs used imply that there was something that was adequately working and now it is necessary to restore, repair, strengthen, and rebuild it; it does not espouse that we need to generate a transformation of the way in which we function or a course adjustment that may result in something different, something better overcoming what existed before. And yet, and very rightly indeed, later on the statement proclaims that the entire effort will be aimed to "underpin prosperity and build an inclusive, green, and sustainable recovery". Behold, a statement propounding an adjustment in the course and systemic way of functioning.

At the very heart of the statement there is therefore a sort of tension between two viewpoints: one that seeks to repair and preserve, and another that seeks to transform. This, in a way, was expected because everything that is new is built out of what is in existence. Beware, however: whatever exists is inherently prone to reproduce, while a transformation requires that what is in existence be used to produce changes. It is a normal yet dangerous tension between an existing order that offers mechanisms and experience, and a new and improved order that needs to be strengthened with that experience while being supplied, from the very start, with the instruments required to impact on the directionality of the social and economic processes. In those turbulent and contradictory waters, those who set, lead, and secure the course acquire critical importance.

When we see the figures that will be allocated to finance the development of middle and low-income countries, and compare them to those committed for the recovery of central countries (not to mention the resources devoted to the wars underway and the production of weapons), the expectations for a growth that is capable of knocking down global inequity vanish. This is why in previous paragraphs we stated that shared growth could not mean everyone growing at the same rate but, instead, making it possible for the least advanced to reinforce their development, so that the huge gaps separating us may begin to close.

In other paragraphs, the London Summit statement speaks about the need to "restore global demand". It is certainly necessary to strengthen global demand, but not to bring it back to exactly the same structure it was before the crisis. Because the global demand profile and the consumption pattern mirrored the prevailing concentration of income: some sectors' consumerism coexisted with the indigence of immense majorities. Today, we should promote more extended and responsible consumption patterns. At the same time, we must send new and different signals to the productive apparatus in order to also transform its productive pattern while orienting it towards the G-20's call 'to work together to build an inclusive, green, and sustainable recovery'.

A social and environmentally sustainable economy is possible; it is not just a guiding utopia. There exist a great variety of policies, measures, and new instruments that can be adopted almost immediately in order to speed up the transition into the ecological economy the G20 declaration aspires to. This is the right time to implement them.

In coming articles we will analyze each of the specific measures contained in the London statement, but it is now worth recognizing an inflection point that the G-20 effort managed to generate: faced with the debacle caused by the crisis, all the players involved have been forced to admit that, without political orientation, the economic dynamics might go further off-track. In other words, we can no longer use automatic pilot to set the course and address the big issues, because by originally applying that strategy our difficulties were not solved but rather augmented.

Today the challenge consists in exercising our free will responsibly, taking into consideration the complexity of the contemporary reality and the need to align the multiple legitimate interests converging on any situation. What is now at stake is the directionality of our future as a globalized society. Perhaps oversimplifying the matter, the bottom-line choice is, once again, between restoring what was in existence or prudently and responsibly embarking on its transformation. That is the question.

CHAPTER XIII

To wipe out hypocrisy and indifference

The hypocrisy and indifference of certain corporate leaders hurt; in 2008 they rewarded themselves as if they did not hold a share of responsibility for having generated the crisis*. Would we have done the same had we been in their place? Are mean-spiritedness and selfishness a mere question of opportunity and circumstances, and do they always prevail over responsibility and solidarity? We may need to embark on a profound individual introspection, to look also at our own behaviour before and during the crisis; to assess how we react to adversity. Coming out of the crisis is a collective effort; and it is good to long for a new social course, a more effective, fairer way of functioning. But this is not only achieved through top down approaches; our actions and attitude also count. They count because of the impact they may have on the course of the social processes, and they count because from that interaction to forge the collective destiny, opportunities emerge to reorient our own individual becoming.

---

*   John Thain, former CEO of Merrill Lynch, Martin Sullivan, former CEO of AIG, Lloyd Blankfein, incumbent CEO of Goldman Sachs, Vikran Pandit, CEO of Citigroup, understand that they and their employees did a good job and in spite of the crisis, in 2008 rewarded themselves with bonuses worth in total 18.4 billion dollars. The top executives in these firms lead lavish lifestyles based on those juicy bonuses: weekend mansions, apartments worth in excess of 20 million dollars in exclusive locations, outrageous decoration expenses, and costly private jet flights. One year ago, Thain spent 1.2 million dollars to refurbish and redecorate his office. Last September, after AIG received a multimillion bailout from the government, 70 of its executives met at a California resort and spent 440,000 dollars.

The New York Times reported that New York's Attorney General accused some of Merrill Lynch' s top executives of "executive irresponsibility" for having secretly collected bonuses worth 3.6 billion US dollars at the time it was announced that Merrill Lynch would receive government aid. Four top executives are suspected of having received $121 million US dollars and some 696 officers might have obtained perks worth more than one million US dollars in 2008*.

What about the crisis? What about their share of responsibility for having generated it? What type of impunity protects them from acting, from generating excesses while acting indifferently to other people's suffering? Is it again, "behind me the deluge"? How do we put up with their conduct? Did we not see at that time that the king was naked, or did we see it and say nothing? Was it that those who spoke out or denounce them were gagged or marginalized socially or economically? Would we have done the same had we been in the place of those corporate leaders? Are mean-spiritedness and selfishness a mere question of opportunity and circumstances, and do they always prevail over responsibility and solidarity? Does this imply that the "other" does not matter, that there are disposable individuals whom we choose to get rid of without much further ado?

Much remains to be explained about the causes that generated the crisis, and from Opinion Sur we join those who seek to understand what happened. It is not a question of assigning the blame or arrogating truths; we need to understand what happened in order to be able to adjust the course and improve our way of functioning as we go along. Yet, even though it is critical that we develop strategic thinking, unveil what is unknown, and explore new courses of action, it is also critical that we embark on a profound individual introspection and wipe ourselves clean from hypocrisy and indifference. We need to turn our eyes toward our own behaviour, before and during the crisis; assess how we react to adversity and whether we have chosen to move ahead alone or extend our hand to those around us.

Coming out of the crisis is a collective effort; and it is good to long for a new social course, a more effective, fairer way of functioning. But this is not achieved through only top down approaches or from

* *Los CEO no se ajustan el cinturón*, a story by Natalia Fabeni published in La Nación, Argentina, on February, 23, 2009.

large social forces down to each individual; the actions, the attitude of each one of us also count. They count because of the impact they may have on the course of the social processes, and they count because from that interaction to forge the collective destiny, opportunities emerge to reorient our own individual becoming.

CHAPTER XIV

The Boiler of Change: Needs, Interests, Values and Emotions

The effort to create a transformation that is aimed at establishing a new course and ensure that the process is viable must emerge from the needs, interests, values and emotions of all social groups, while sorting through possibilities and restrictions in the pursuit of outcomes that are, to a great extent, uncertain. A complex process is the one that bubbles up in the boiler of change.

The detrimental situations we would like to change are many and varied, and so are the ways in which we react to them. In some cases we do not act upon causes and, instead, try to avoid consequences; in other situations we attempt to make adjustments in order to mitigate effects; only on certain occasions do we embark on the process of building a transformation.

Creating a transformation involves many things. To begin with, a key aspect of its construction has to do with the direction of the intended transformation. The viability of the process is equally important because the willingness to generate a transformation is not sufficient in and of itself: it is also necessary to take into account the local and surrounding circumstances, possibilities, and restrictions that condition the viability of any change or that might render outcomes impossible to anticipate with any amount of certainty.

Direction and viability are intrinsically related. When we set a course, we have a certain idea about its attainability, and such viability will be influenced by the nature and intensity of the changes made in direction that the new course requires.

The construction of transformation occurs within a context of multiple players interacting with one another; each of them having their own needs, their own values, and their own changing interests and emotions. It is a complex process, the one that bubbles up in the boiler of change.

Even if we acknowledge how complex it is to change the present, no situation remains unchanged with the course of time: every situation is ever-changing, sometimes in hardly noticeable homeopathic doses, sometimes through quantum leaps, yet mostly at slow, yet sustained, steps. There is no uniform transformation pace; instead, there exists periods of acceleration, slow-progress or deceleration. The current period seems to be a one of accelerated transformation.

WHAT WE CARRY IN OUR BACKPACKS

Good walkers that we are, we carry backpacks. We usually load them with needs, interests, values and emotions.

(I) Complex and changing needs

An improvement in well being is associated with the satisfaction of needs, this simple expression hides however, more than what it shows. There are many and diverse types of needs, some of them basic necessities such as feeding ourselves, taking shelter, communicating, and security, while among others that are essential to the human condition, such as overcoming helplessness, obtaining recognition and affection, and ensuring one's dignity as an individual. This list is only an example of the vast and diverse universe of needs, which, in addition, vary according to social sector, place, age group, gender, etc.

Necessities have an objective, as well as a subjective, dimension, the latter involving how each one perceives and feels them. Nor do they become stagnated: they evolve as new knowledge thresholds and more effective satisfiers are obtained. What is considered a satisfactory level is permanently displaced, an understandable fact that implies having to always live with a certain dose of dissatisfaction. This contributes to displacing over time any goal regarding coverage of necessities that any plan or program may have adopted.

(II) The load of interests

In addition to needs, our backpacks are loaded with changing interests that evolve hand in hand with the needs and urges that drive all human beings. There exist a diversity of interests, some of them being more central than others and felt more or less strongly, crudely, moderately or susceptible of being sublimated according to values and emotions.

The social dynamics generates a flow of situations, in each of which a variety of interests struggle to be heard, prevail, or, on occasions, just survive. In this struggle, it is the strongest and/or best-organized players who tend to prevail.

Interests are expressed and, in turn, channeled through an extensive set of social and economic institutions and regulations. This institutional framework is the result of agreements and impositions decanting throughout history. When institutions are not capable of amalgamating interests, struggles mount into confrontations that are settled by non-institutional means.

(III) Values

We also carry values in our backpacks. They are principles and rules we have inherited from earlier generations or acquired throughout our own life. Each one tends to believe that their values are true and universal. In fact, however, there are billions of value bearers acting in very different contexts of needs and interests. And even though there are widely accepted values that are inherent to the dignity of the human condition, their interpretation and implementation differ enormously from place to place and situation to situation; they are forced to change and become adjusted to the course of time and the evolution of our societies.

This does not ignore the critical role that values play as a supplement and moderation factor of individual interests that move us away from the law of the jungle and the notion of "every man for himself". But it also sends a warning about the manipulation of values aimed at smuggling other interests that, otherwise, would not be supported in the open. Special mention should be made as to the many types of fundamentalisms that deem their own values as superior and claim to be the sole owners of the truth, always.

(IV) Emotions

The heart or minds of those who carry backpacks are ancestrally stirred by emotions that may help or harm our way forward. Emotions contribute to strengthening our motivation and mobilization for action, but they may also disturb or confuse our reasoning. Emotions add vibration to our determination, exalting the value of what is ours. They are indispensable to build a transformation, but it is necessary to see that they do not cloud the process of setting appropriate courses and the effort to ensure the viability of the process.

Being a part of human nature, emotions cannot be ignored; they are and will be with us forever. But their inherent frailty should keep us on the alert so that we call upon them constructively and avoid that they be used for destruction.

SETTING THE COURSE AND REORIENTING OUR WAY FORWARD

We now see the complexity involved in setting a certain societal course and ensuring the viability of the intended transformation. In essence, transformation is a construction process where we control some variables within certain parameters that condition the course and viability but, paradoxically, also end up being affected by the dynamics of the process they condition. Building transformation requires identifying and weighting a vast array of social needs, interests, values, and emotions, based on a mid and long-term projection that is devised in order to secure the support of those who are called to redirect their way forward.

Reorienting the course is a collective effort that is faced at all levels; at neighborhoods and towns, at spaces where specialists and the ordinary citizen try to understand reality, at political and governmental instances, in the world of business as well as civil society organizations, in the sphere of education and the media. From that social magma there emerge inspiring visions and utopias that give way to initiatives, plans and actions that materialize the course.

To be successful, the effort of building a transformation requires generating synergies and supplementing efforts while keeping as far away as possible from antagonisms that might deviate and sterilize energies. This is no easy task because it will be necessary to convince those who will eventually benefit from such changes while, at the same time overcome the resistances of those who might be threatened by them. Some resistances are based on very plausible reasons and others, on spurious interests; some are held in good faith, while there are others that purposefully struggle to preserve new and old privileges.

The process of creating a transformation takes place at several stages that, even though may have sufficient entity and are singular enough to be recognized as such, are never the less part of a number of complementary efforts. This includes interpreting what is going on, projecting aspirations towards attainable mid and-long term goals, stimulating the convergence of interests, and mobilizing willingness and organizing action. If this is to occur, the intended transformation cannot be achieved without impacting on critical aspects of social, economic, and political functioning. It is in this sense that that the transformation we want is not dreamed or awaited, but worked on.

CHAPTER XV

From Inequality to Responsibility

It is not just a question of abating inequality and enhancing the access to opportunities, but also of exalting social, political, environmental responsibility. What would be the point in overcoming the opprobrium of inequality, to then fall into that of social, environmental and political irresponsibility? The passage from inequality to equality is a necessary, yet not sufficient, condition to ensure sustainable development; it must be attained but, in doing so, values and attitudes will have to be changed. Responsibility brings along a new series of criteria that guide and straighten up individual behavior that has nothing to do with launching to the market a new wave of destroyers of the environment, social harmony, respect for the other, and cooperation with the rest.

Fortunately, the notion that it is necessary to abate inequality is ever more present in citizen awareness as well as in the political agenda. This is already a step forward in respect to continuing to live in very unequal societies as though this is something natural, permanent, or inevitable. In those societies, citizens are concerned about their own well being, but anesthetized about what happens to the others; they lock the other way and ignore the complex relations bonding us all, sensitive –if they ever are– to only their families and their closest friends. The rest, that immense universe of other human beings, is considered just a part of the context within which we have to live.

However, anyone who is able to stand above ignorance and stupidity knows that others' circumstances, in one way or another, directly or indirectly influences what happens to us. When inequality prevails, not only those who lag behind are abandoned, but also the functioning of society as a whole becomes affected.

In previous chapters we specified how inequality disrupts the benefits of organic growth; how an ever more segmented effective demand becomes out phased in respect to a vigorous productive supply encouraged by today's tremendous technological development; how income concentration also expresses itself in the concentration of savings; how investment is deviated from the real economy toward financial speculation; how, in this process, avarice is exacerbated and risks are hidden; how the pattern of consumption becomes ever more superfluous and how advertising spreads it to society as a whole; how the economic system seeks to avoid market strangling by resorting not to improving genuine income but, rather, to consumer indebtedness; how we then fall into a perilous over-indebtedness that leads to the creation of tremendous financial bubbles, until there comes a day when they burst, with devastating effects. We also mentioned that such economic processes correlate at the political level by upholding institutions that favor that particular type of functioning, and that certain strategic think tanks justify the prevailing order ignoring the debacle germinating below the surface.

A growth such as the one described above –concentration oriented, anchored to each one's own interest, successful for some and indifferent to the suffering of others– generates values, ideas, attitudes, and behaviors that render its reproduction possible. The obvious question is how huge majorities can be subjected to that situation and its demolishing effects.

The answers are diverse, as diverse are the circumstances and the history of each specific situation. There are cultures where resignation to the established order, and respect for traditional authority, is rooted in beliefs and traditions. There are few societies where political, economic and communicational power are connected and complement one another functionally. Some communities were disarticulated as such by bloody dictatorships, ethnic conflicts, or natural catastrophes; others fled their milieu for economic reasons and are vulnerable migrants in foreign land; a number of them became subjected by minorities with greater coercive power.

In any situation there coexist persons and organizations having very diverse needs, interests, values and emotions; this is always the case. We live in essentially heterogeneous contexts, sometimes with deep and apparently irreconcilable differences, and at other times, only diverse in terms of nuances. The point is that such diversity exists and, in spite of attempts at eliminating it, it persists and is reproduced with the course of time because it is inherent to the nature of human groups.

It is then difficult to explain how, notwithstanding the lessons taught by the long and painful history of humanity, we keep wanting to eliminate the other one, or force him or her to be like us; subduing and submitting him rather than reconciling interests and needs, working to attain convergences, seeking complementarities, identifying synergies and new ways to help, and respecting and preserving the diversity of individualities.

When the different types and forms of democratic systems emerged, a ray of hope was cast. In democracy, differences of interests, conflicts and tensions inherent to the social functioning are addressed and sought to be resolved by peaceful means, through agreements that are, sometimes, generous and entail detachment and, at other times, result in very tough "give-and-takes". The problem is that democracies are imperfect, and many times they preserve profound injustices and inequalities within.

This may perhaps correspond to a certain phase in the development of democracies in which they are more formal than full-fledged; democracies where privilege-entrenched interests with considerable means resist changes that might give way to greater equality and social harmony. One of the main challenges of the 21st century is to preserve democracies by rooting them in social and economic terms; to defend individual rights founded on the freedom of conscience that was so hard to conquer, while securing social justice and greater equality of opportunities for all without any discrimination whatsoever.

Today this aspiration lies in abating inequality among and within countries, and in eliminating poverty and indigence altogether wherever they may be found. A goal on which it is easy to agree but the resolution of which raises controversy because, in order to overcome resistance, it is indispensable that we embark on the complex task of aligning those above-mentioned multiple and diverse interests, needs, values and emotions. Besides, it is not just a question of going from inequality to equality but in addition to exalting social, political, and environmental responsibility. What would be the point in overcoming the opprobrium of inequality, to then fall into social, environmental and political irresponsibility? The passage from inequality to equality is a necessary, yet not sufficient, condition to ensure sustainable development. Certainly, it must be attained, but in doing so, the behavior of persons should also be changed, both of those who benefited from inequality as well as those who will access the opportunities they had been previously deprived of.

Responsibility brings along a new series of criteria that guide and improve individual behavior. We would be doing sustainable development a small favor if we bring to the market a new wave of destroyers of the environment, social harmony, respect for the other, and cooperation with the rest.

CHAPTER XVI

Abating Inequality to Find a Sustainable Way out of the Crisis

Creating a way out of the crisis that leads to a sustainable development and is adjusted to the circumstances of each country and each community is feasible and necessary. These ways out are defined by a complex, imperfect, and changing decision-making structure that culminate at the political level. The new course and way of functioning should be expressed in a consistent set of macroeconomic measures and mesoeconomic practices, as well as in the creation of a support system targeted towards the bottom of the social and economic pyramid. As new ideas germinate in the individual and collective conscience, there is a gradual transformation of the set of values prevailing in each society, which is what will ultimately ensure the sustenance and perdurability of the new course.

In previous articles we analyzed how the economic concentration process, with its impact on inequality and poverty, prevented organic growth and thus contributed to generating the circumstances that led to the present global crisis. In these lines we mention some of the key measures that may be taken to abate inequality and poverty and, hence, exit the crisis towards sustainable development.

THE EFFECTS OF CONCENTRATION

In organic growth, the level and structure of effective demand accompany and absorb that which a vibrant productive apparatus produces. When this

111

balance becomes affected by concentration-oriented growth, causing the income of middle and low income sectors to lag strongly behind the supply, one possible way of addressing this imbalance is through credit: consumers do not get better income but, instead, become indebted. It is clear that if the relative income-lag is not eliminated, sooner or later over-indebtedness will be incurred, which is precisely what happened in this crisis. Dangerous financial bubbles were born and inflated, until one day they burst and swept away the financial system that made them possible (and profited from them) and then, in a domino effect, affected the rest of the economic system and the various sectors of the real economy.

Concentrating growth prevailed almost all over the world and expressed itself not only in that gap between the genuine income of middle and lower sectors and the productive apparatus' supply. There were many other effects, such as the concentration of savings and its channeling into financial products of high though concealed risk; the greed and loss of boundaries of some financial operators; the deliberate or negligent complicity of a great deal of national and international public regulators; investment concentration on certain nodes of the economic system that increased the divorce between high technology and efficiency segments, and a huge and more and more marginalized universe of small and micro producers.

At the same time, the concentration of income altered the profile of the demand, and with it, the signs given to the productive apparatus regarding the type of production it should offer. Superfluous consumption grew amid the affluent sectors, a consumption matrix the media advertised and enticed to the increasingly indebted middle sectors. Rather than responsible consumption, exacerbated consumerism prevailed, which augmented the already accelerated environmental destruction. The consumerist zeal ignored the debacle of many families, ruptured protective networks, and favored the addiction epidemic and the alienated search for substitute happiness.

The effects of economic concentration did not stop there, as a greater concentration of political and communicational power was generated with a strong propensity to the homogenization of strategic thinking. Concentrated financial resources, as well as access to the also concentrated information and idea dissemination channels, were allocated with greater generosity to strategic think tanks akin to income concentration interests.

These statements are not related to any ideological or partisan radicalism whatsoever. The fact of the matter is that the systemic effects of a certain way of functioning expand and spread, affecting almost all levels and corners of society, the economy, politics, education, the environment, values, interpersonal relationships, and our own individual psychology. None of those categories are truly isolated spheres but rather dimensions –influencing one another in a sole and complex reality.

TRANSFORMING TO ENSURE SUSTAINABLE DEVELOPMENT

We need to distinguish the factors that can be changed in the short run from those that are either not possible to change or require more time in order to be fully transformed. We can thus acknowledge the limits and restrictions in which we are operating, yet at the same time notice the possibility of acting and of implementing our free will and determination with realism. We must now move forward, exposed to the risk of falling in irresponsible voluntarism, on the one hand and, on the other one, in paralyzing determinism.

How can we then deploy, in a context of crisis, transforming actions that are capable of abating concentration, inequity and poverty, and give way to a new systemic course?

In the first place, it should be acknowledged that efforts aimed to abate concentration, inequality, and poverty, are not marginal actions that merely "supplement" central decisions. There is no point in deploying macroeconomic measures and mesoeconomic initiatives that overlook the key purpose of transforming the concentration process and then, as an ineffective yet attention-getting salute to the flag, put forth a "special program" aimed to eradicate inequality and poverty. Nothing could be farther from what is needed to implement a course change.

In order to forge a path out of the crisis aimed at sustainable development, it is necessary to simultaneously work on macroeconomic policies, mesoeconomic actions and measures of direct support to the base of the social pyramid. All of this must be coupled with the critical effort of modifying attitudes and values and indispensable social and political pillars to ensure a sustainable trajectory.

(I) Macroeconomic action to find a sustainable way out

To ensure a sustainable way out of the crisis, the set of macroeconomic policies must converge with the goal of energizing the economy by transforming the concentration-oriented growth pattern, eradicating inequality and exclusion, and mobilizing the base of the production apparatus. To attain this, it will be necessary to make full use of fiscal policy, public spending policy, monetary and credit policy, investment policy, and science and technology policy, among several others.

As far as fiscal policy is concerned, it is critical that the regressive biases that are typical of almost all of our tax systems be corrected. Regardless of the fact that some taxes are easier to collect than others, the guiding criterion to eradicate inequality is that those who have least pay proportionally less and not more than the most affluent ones, as it happens today. Evasion and corruption aggravate the unfairness of an unequal tax burden. These are not unconnected phenomena; it must be made clear that if evasion and corruption are not tackled, in addition to perverting the social system of rewards and punishments, inequality and poverty eradication efforts become diluted.

Public spending is another key variable to correct and transform the concentration process and eradicate inequality. It is usually the main funding source of social and production infrastructure and, as such, it must be allocated with systemic efficacy and social justice while prioritizing those sectors that are lagging behind. To meet the legitimate needs of middle-high and high-income sectors, private funding may be used but without using public funds, as it happens many times today.

In addition, it is essential to adopt a monetary policy that ensures price stability: it is well known that instability more severely hits those who are most defenseless –the low and middle– income sectors. Within a context of monetary stability, credit may be oriented so that it flows abundantly and properly to the bottom of the production pyramid and strengthens the financial intermediaries capable of managing their small loan portfolios with the rigor and responsibility that the case requires.

A serious situation in our countries is that there does not exist an investment policy favoring the critical formation of capital in micro and small production ventures. It is necessary to establish incentives and regulatory frameworks favoring the creation of instruments that may channel capital, knowledge, contacts and information to the bottom of the productive apparatus, similar to the ones proposed in (III).

In economies that are increasingly knowledge dependent, scientific and technological production becomes one of the most important strategic variables. It is necessary to gear that production so that it serves sustainable development and takes very special care of the base of the productive apparatus.

(II) Mesoeconomic action

Coordinately with macroeconomic policies, mesoeconomic action is required from production chain-leading firms who are co-responsible for materializing a sustainable course and enhancing systemic functioning. This critical role of leading firms is not usually duly valued and yet, a good portion of the potential for transforming organic growth lies in the ill-defined mesoeconomic spaces of production networks.

Large corporations must take into account the impact that their decisions have on the other players within the production network they lead. This implies ensuring sustainability to suppliers, distributors, and those who buy their products; be these supplies, capital goods or consumer goods. This is about fostering, in the companies, a systemic vision of their own development, so as to minimize negative externalities and use the positive ones for the benefit of their whole productive network and the communities they operate in.

(III) Direct support to the base of the social pyramid

A third strategic axis consists in establishing an effective micro, small and medium-sized entrepreneur support system. In this set of economic players lies a little-recognized reservoir of talent and determination to mobilize in full the production potential of a community. The support system is aimed at generating the conditions required for entrepreneurs to be able to operate within contexts of excellence and efficacy, favoring access to top-level (not residual or scrap) knowledge, contacts, modern business engineering, intelligent capital, and the values of solidarity and responsibility towards others and the environment.

It was already pointed out that to come out of the crisis and move towards sustainable development it is critical that a vigorous formation of capital at the bottom of the production apparatus be generated, which does not involve reproducing at that level socially and environmentally irresponsible behaviors. It is not a question of extending social injustice or environmental destruction to the farthest productive limit or border. We would be doing no favor to sustainable development by launching into the market millions of irresponsible new production units. The paradigm of the selfish producer, indifferent to the social and environmental milieu is not the only possible one. It was imposed by a particular manner of functioning where the individual quest was excessively privileged over the quest of society as a whole. Today it is necessary to preserve individual initiative and rights, in addition to imposing duties of responsibility towards others and the planet. To that end, it will be necessary to establish policies, regulations, attitudes and relations among players that may promote the formation of "responsible capital" at the bottom of the productive apparatus. It is possible to attain this –and we know how to do it– by using a new generation of small and micro producer support institutions.

By reinforcing the profile of the responsible entrepreneur there is an enhanced social recognition of the role of the production organizer that mobilizes our productive factors. An effective support system will help small entrepreneurs embark on more promising production opportunities using the best and most modern business engineering; at the same time, it will orient them so that their actions may impact positively on the local economy. This implies sharing economic and technological results both with the small units workers and, when creating modern mid size organizations on the basis of integrating small production that is now scattered, with those who decide to get together in order to access better opportunities. It also entails sharing results with the local governments that will access additional fiscal resources generated by the expansion of the tax base.

The support system encompasses a battery of new promotion instruments including inclusive business developers, socially and environmentally responsible investor angel networks, and local funds to support productive investment, assistance agreements made with technological institutes, and business schools and entrepreneurial management consulting firms.

An effective support system acknowledges the central role of entrepreneurs to whom backing is provided, and focuses on developing businesses that are inclusive. Few are the entrepreneurs who surface from the swamp of poverty, and even worse, indigent, without any help. The pain of families that are now marginalized from growth is huge and the executive capacity that is being wasted, gigantic.

It is worth cautioning against the risk of establishing ghettos made up only of small entrepreneurs instead of integrating people with disparate backgrounds, education, and access to information and contacts. Segregating the poor or the marginalized does not productively contribute to a transformation of their reality; rather, it tends to reproduce the conditions in which they usually operate. A more effective way of overcoming shortages and gaining access to new, better opportunities is to partner up small and micro producers with other players that may supplement and empower them, and do this on the basis of fair relations with shared responsibility. This is a vast field to explore, one in which the support system plays a crucial role because with its resources and assistance it sets courses and proposes ways of functioning. Certainly, this promising field is not tension-free because there are many and diverse interests converging on inclusive ventures.

(IV) Adjusting attitudes and values

Coming out of the crisis towards sustainable development is not a technocratic fact but an essentially social, political and individual process. In fact, there are different ways out of a crisis, and each one of them involves establishing different relations among the members of a community, a country, the global village. The decision-making structure prevailing in each situation tries to take up individual wills and, considering parameters and limitations, sets the course and rules of procedure.

It is a fact that the decision-making power is not equally distributed; instead, some have more capacity than others to impact on strategic decision-making. These asymmetries are founded on economic and political participation differences, on media control, and on extended processes of conscience alienation. Hence, to deepen our imperfect democracies it will be indispensable to eradicate inequality and poverty, promote political participation, democratize communication, and tackle the alienation that deviates our will from the goals of meaningfulness and development. Social directionality is ultimately established at the political level, but it is sustained with attitudes and values germinating in the individual and collective conscience.

It is always necessary to convince ourselves of the fact that it is possible to try something different from the existent, that no society is immutable; all of them evolve according to the circumstances of their times; that strategic thinking is critical, and that even more critical is our everyday behavior, which give expression to what we are and aspire.

It is of no use rewarding selfishness as if it were the only possible driver of peoples' development. For centuries, the criterion of caring only for one's own self prevailed, but in a globalized world that may be fatal. Today, the individual effort that pursues one's own well being is still legitimate and plausible, as long as it does not affect but rather contributes to the well-being of others and the safety of the planet.

In brief, creating ways out of the crisis leading to a sustainable development adjusted to the circumstances of each country and each community is feasible and necessary. These ways out are defined by a complex, imperfect and changing decision-making structure culminating at the political level. The new course and way of functioning should be expressed in a consistent set of macroeconomic measures and mesoeconomic practices, as well as in the creation of a support system targeted towards the bottom of the social and economic pyramid. As new ideas germinate in the individual and collective conscience, there is a gradual transformation of the set of values prevailing in each society, which is what ultimately will ensure the sustenance and perdurability of the new course.

LOS HILOS DEL DESORDEN
JUAN EUGENIO CORRADI
ISBN: 987-22536-3-3
Publisher: Del Umbral
Pages: 288
Date of Publishing: June 2006
Language: Spanish
Paperback

UN PAÍS PARA TODOS
ROBERTO SANSÓN MIZRAHI
ISBN: 987-22536-4-1
Publisher: Del Umbral
Pages: 240
Date of Publishing: June 2006
Language: Spanish
Paperback

*NEGOCIOS LOCALES
OPORTUNIDADES GLOBALES*
EDUARDO REMOLINS
ISBN: 978-987-1408-0-9
Publisher: Del Umbral
pages: 144
Date of Publishing: August 2007
Language: Spanish
Paperback

www.ingramcontent.com/pod-product-compliance
Lightning Source LLC
Chambersburg PA
CBHW072204280526
45788CB00002B/869